The Patriarchy of Shakespeare's Comedies

The Patriarchy of Shakespeare's Comedies

MARILYN L. WILLIAMSON

Wayne State University Press, Detroit, 1986

Library of Congress Cataloging-in-Publication Data

Williamson, Marilyn L., 1927–
  The patriarchy of Shakespeare's comedies.

  Bibliography: p.
  Includes index.
  1. Shakespeare, William, 1564–1616—Comedies.
2. Patriarchy in literature.   3. Shakespeare, William,
1564–1616—Political and social views.   4. Politics and
literature.   I. Title.
PR2981.W495   1986   822.3'3   86-11151
ISBN 0-8143-1807-X

Grateful acknowledgment is made to the Mary Dickey Masterton Publication Fund for
financial assistance in the publication of this volume.

To the Memory of My Father

CONTENTS

ACKNOWLEDGMENTS

The general argument and versions of two chapters of this book have been presented at scholarly meetings. Chapter One had its first incarnation as "Courtship into Marriage: Cuckoldry and the Power of Women in the Middle Comedies" and was read by a seminar on gender and genre chaired by Coppelia Kahn at the International Shakespeare Congress, Stratford-upon-Avon, in August 1981. The first version of Chapter Two, "Sexuality, Patriarchy, and Marriage in *Measure* and *All's Well*," was presented in a seminar on sexuality in the problem plays, chaired by Paul Merrix at the Shakespeare Association Convention, Ashland, Oregon, in April 1983. The general argument of the study was read as "Sexuality and Social Constraint in Shakespeare's Comedies" to a special session on sexuality and gender in Shakespeare, organized by Judith K. Gardiner at the Modern Language Association Convention in Washington, D. C., in December 1984. I am grateful to participants at these conventions for helpful suggestions about my work. Thanks are due to the students in my Shakespeare courses for many years, but most especially to those in the graduate seminar devoted to "Sex and Power in Shakespeare's Comedies" during fall semester 1984. Their agreement confirmed my views, but, more than that, their differences sharpened my understanding.

I wish also to thank Professor Marianne Novy and an anonymous reader of the whole manuscript for valuable criticism. For their advice and encouragement at various stages, I wish to acknowledge Bernard Goldman, Richard Kinney, and especially Robert Mandel, successive directors of the Wayne State University Press. Anne Adamus has been very helpful in the final preparations of the manuscript.

For the time necessary to revise the manuscript and prepare it for publication, I wish to thank the Educational Foundation of the American Association of University Women for the Michigan Fellowship in 1983–84, Wayne State University for a sabbatical semester in 1984, and the Department of English, Wayne State University, for the Josephine Nevins Keal Chair for 1985–86.

I am deeply grateful to George Masterton of the Purdy Library at Wayne State for his unfailing aid in obtaining materials and finding answers to numerous troublesome queries, and most especially for selecting this book for support from the Mary Dickey Masterton Publication Fund.

Thanks are also due to friends, notably Mary Bolton, Jeanne Flood, Carole Herhold, Pearl Warn, and my son, Timothy Williamson, for conversation and encouragement. Although I have been asked not to, I will thank James H. McKay for his unshakable faith in whatever I do.

INTRODUCTION

This book is a study of power relationships in Shakespeare's comedies: it is made possible by new assumptions about the study of history and the study of literature. First, there is a new perception of power, which emerges from feminist thought[1] and from post-structuralists like Michel Foucault. For such thinkers power does not reside just in the state or even in explicit social structures as such:

> Power must be analysed as something which circulates, or rather as something which only functions in the form of a chain. It is never localised here or there, never in anybody's hands, never appropriated as a commodity or piece of wealth. Power is employed or exercised through a net-like organisation. And not only do individuals circulate between its threads; they are always in the position of simultaneously undergoing and exercising this power. They are not only its inert or consenting target; they are always also the elements of its articulation. In other words, individuals are the vehicles of power, not its points of application.[2]

From such a perspective power exists in relationships—all relationships. So the capacity of a Renaissance wife to make her husband a cuckold—because she is his property—is a form of power: his very possession of her invests her with power. It is fascinating to discover that because Renaissance political thinkers refused to make the modern distinction between the state and society, their definitions of power are closer to Foucault's than those after Hobbes and Locke, closer because they rest first in family relationships.[3] Therefore recent thinking about power enables us to read Renaissance political discourse and literary representations of power with greater appreciation than heretofore.

Our new definitions of power also give us access to its representation in comedies, a genre not usually associated with politics. Although certain comedies, such as *Measure for Measure,* have obvious political themes, most comedies have not been assumed by critics to be political because they dealt with private themes as they were defined in the Renaissance and by general practice ever since. Tragedies, those plays which represent kings and public actions, are plays of state and power. With our new interest in sexual politics and power relationships within the family, we may now understand comedic actions as representing power in ways that were significant in Shakespeare's time and in our own as well.

My method of approaching the plays has been through their historical context. Here again definitions have recently changed. Formerly, historical studies of literature assumed that each era had a distinctive set of beliefs from which it produced literature and that these beliefs could be ascertained largely from intellectual history—from the study of philosophical and religious texts that could then be shown to be influences or sources for works of literature. Just as literary works contained central themes, so historical eras spoke with one voice, accompanied by an occasional undertone or overtone. Now literary scholars who use history as a context stress the complexity and multiplicity of any historical moment and the changes that take place within eras formerly regarded as relatively stable.[4] Any historical moment is conceived as one in which ideas and ideologies are living, dying, and struggling to be born. Recent studies have made us aware, for example, of the social mobility in an Elizabethan society which represented itself most frequently as a fixed social hierarchy.[5] The family, once monolithic, now has an increasingly complex history,[6] and women, once comfortably ignored, have become as various as Cleopatra.[7]

The contextual critic does not search only for sources that may be directly linked to a literary text for two reasons. The first is that this approach does not assume that literature reproduces literally aspects of the historical moment, which has a greater "reality" imitated by art.[8] Therefore topical references are not an object of inquiry. Instead, this method assumes that literature represents reality according to systems of cultural language that take the place of the referent. The historical critic seeks to understand the codes of that language and connect those to the representations within specific works. The method requires, therefore, connecting a given text to a wide range of cultural artifacts—marriage manuals, jokes, diaries, political tracts, sermons, parliamentary debates, cony-catching pamphlets, royal proclamations, court records—to understand both the culture and the language in which it could make representations. That language will always be understood to embody ideology in both its contemporary senses.[9] That is, ideology is, on the one hand, a cultural system of beliefs which perpetuate the dominant power structure, and, on the other, the social practices by which any culture conducts life and the terms in which it perceives its world. Study of history allows us to perceive the ideologies of other ages than our own and thereby to deconstruct what to other ages seemed largely transparent and natural. Recent studies have revealed how self-conscious Renaissance thinkers were about "custom," which we would call ideology today.[10] In its broader sense ideology cannot be separated from language itself, and in its narrower sense it is essential in dealing with issues of power, the focus of this

book. And it is especially useful in dealing with patriarchal
ideas in Shakespeare's romances, where the genre permits a
representation of political structures as natural.

A second reason contextual criticism does not seek to
connect specific sources with literary texts is that it does not
privilege literature and place the historical context as a background to it. Instead, the historical critic investigates "both
the social presence to the world of the literary text and the
presence of the world in the literary text."[11] A consequence
of this orientation is the study of the ways in which audiences
of different epochs may "use" literature to deal with anxieties, frustrations, problems presented them by their worlds.
Part of the argument of this study is that romantic comedy of
successful courtship of a powerful woman and a profitable
marriage was an attractive fantasy for the generation that
came to maturity in the "bottleneck years," the 1590s, when
there were too few opportunities at court and in professions
for a surplus of able, educated men. As the next generation
matured, much more numerous and better educated than
their parents, their well-to-do elders became anxious about
the young people's marriage choices, and, after the Petrarchan fantasies lost their meaning, a spate of dramas of
enforced marriage appears in the first decade of the seventeenth century. The plays are history, not as literal tran-
scripts of their moment, but as representations of "women
on top"[12] or the ruler as a nurturing father to his subjects.[13]
The drama responds to James's succession of Elizabeth and
to their styles of ruling.

If literature is not privileged by historical critics, it is also
not assumed to be the voice of the dominant ideology. By
stressing the unity of the text, critics in the past had become
"the accomplice of ideology." In finding the coherence of the
work, such critics seek "a way of repairing any deficiencies in
consistency by reference to the author's philosophy or contemporary world picture. . . . Having created a canon of acceptable texts, criticism then provides them with acceptable
interpretations, thus effectively censoring any elements in
them which come into collision with the dominant ide-

ology."[14] Encouraged by a sense of the complexity of the historical moment, with its conflicting and inconsistent ideologies and varied conditions, the historical critic will examine the way in which a given text may support, interrogate, or subvert the dominant ideology. The ways in which the romantic comedies contain the power of women are good examples here: in *As You Like It* Rosalind's power is temporary and contained in the structure of the play; in *Much Ado* Beatrice's conversion of Benedick interrogates the conventional conclusion of the main plot; in *Merchant* Portia's continuing power subverts her subordination in marriage. Asking such questions about texts reveals how, for example, the drama of enforced marriage reconciles males to the patriarchy's constraints on their desire, or how children in the romances are destined to serve the state, even when they rebel.

Because history is not a background to the literary text but a context, the historical material is presented with analysis of the related themes and structures within the plays. Thus, the historical materials form an intertextual field in which the plays may be situated and read, but without the assumption that Shakespeare is imitating a prior historical reality. He is simply using the language of his time. His plays also form their own intertextual field, and so they are read together as groups according to their subgenres: *Merchant of Venice, Much Ado, As You Like It,* and *Twelfth Night* as comedies of courtship; *All's Well* as a drama of enforced marriage and *Measure* as a play of the disguised ruler; and the romances *Pericles, Cymbeline, Winter's Tale,* and *The Tempest.* Because Shakespeare experimented with a variety of comedic genres in his early period, those plays have been omitted from discussion, except for *Love's Labour's Lost,* an early version of the comedy of courtship. Of the early comedies, *Midsummer Night's Dream* is the one which holds great interest for the critic studying power relationships historically, as Louis A. Montrose demonstrates in a recent essay.[15] I will not repeat Montrose's argument except to say that he elucidates the complex intertexuality of the play and Theseus's and Obe-

ron's coercion of Hippolyta and Titania. In the terms presented here, *Midsummer Night's Dream* anticipates the problem plays, for it represents two rulers who seek to regulate
sexuality and a bed trick in which Oberon successfully manipulates Titania's desires to make them accord with his own.
Troilus and Cressida and *Henry VIII* have been omitted from
their possible groups because they depart substantially from
the subgenres and so their special characteristics would
therefore be more distorted than illuminated by this technique of reading. Shakespeare's plays are read against one
another for the same reason that the problem plays are read
against their subgenres: they illuminate differences through
sameness. For example, after understanding the dynamics of
the drama of enforced marriage in *All's Well,* we are better
able to assess the instabilities of the marriages at the end of
Measure. Without that perspective, a critic might feel uneasy
about the relationships, but dismiss the unions among the
conventions of comedy. Its differences from the other romances allow us to use *The Tempest* in understanding how the
earlier romances mythologize power structures, making
them seem natural and inevitable. Thus, groups of plays and
the historical material effectively decenter any particular
text.

The limitations of all these procedures should be acknowledged. No single play is ever given a consistent, thorough reading. In fact, the goal is not necessarily to provide
new readings—though they may result—but to offer a new
historical perspective on the plays and to understand themes
heretofore neglected. Therefore, institutional structures,
cultural codes, and personal relationships are connected to
the subgenres of the plays and to the context. This is not a
criticism that deals extensively with character, and some
important themes, such as usury in *Merchant* or religion in
Measure, are simply ignored for the common themes and
structures that these techniques illuminate. The aim of the
criticism is to demonstrate the contingency of the representations of power in the comedies and thereby to contribute to

the feminist controversy about Shakespeare's representations of women and patriarchy.

It is no secret that Shakespeare has been the focus of considerable disagreement among feminist critics, beginning with Juliet Dusinberre's *Shakespeare and the Nature of Women*.[16] On the one hand, we have Dusinberre or Irene Dash presenting a Shakespeare whose portraits of women "extended beyond his own sex and beyond his own time."[17] For such critics Shakespeare is a protofeminist. For Marilyn French or Linda Bamber, on the other hand, Shakespeare inevitably wrote from a male perspective.[18] Both employ universalized models of male and female, Self and Other, to read a variety of Shakespeare's plays, tracing changes in gender relationships according to genre. Neither critic attempts to relate her model to history. Although her work is much more sophisticated as to cultural codes, Coppelia Kahn's psychoanalytic studies also emphasize the universal in the male struggle for identity and separation from the mother. In this reading the patriarchal society of his time "simply exacerbated male anxieties about identity."[19] For Kahn, too, Shakespeare is a protofeminist in questioning the cultural definitions of sexual identity in his times. If one accepts these critics' view that Shakespeare represents the universal human condition in his plays, then the need of all these critics to discover their values in Shakespeare becomes clear: if he is universal, he has always been there before us.

It seems almost inevitable that such feminist criticism should be answered by those who question its premises, and so Lisa Jardine's *Still Harping on Daughters* was quickly followed by Linda Woodbridge's *Women and the English Renaissance*. Both books relate literary representation to the historical context and both deal with literature beyond Shakespeare, but Jardine writes specifically to answer the critics described above: "I try to suggest alternative (corrective) possibilities for reading the relationship between real social conditions, and literary representation." Jardine therefore includes a wide variety of historical texts, which she hopes future students may use in connection with the drama of Shakespeare's age. Yet, despite its title, Jardine's book is like other feminist criticism in privileging women as the focus of study: "This book is directed at the reader who comes to Shakespeare's drama with a special interest in his female characters."[20]

With few exceptions feminist critics concentrate on women, probably because of their relative neglect, and scant the other term in the feminist paradigm: patriarchy. For feminist writers in general, patriarchy is a code term for all those structures in any society which oppress women. In fact, as Veronica Beechey has pointed out, feminist theory has neglected development of the concept of patriarchy: "None of the existing literature provides a satisfactory way of conceptualizing patriarchy." At the end of her fine essay "On Patriarchy," Beechey calls for historical investigation of patriarchal institutions: "First, I think a satisfactory theory of patriarchy should be historically specific and should explore the forms of patriarchy which exist within particular modes of production. This would suggest that the forms of patriarchy which exist in capitalism are different from the forms of patriarchy existing in pre-capitalist or socialist societies."[21] Such study has particular importance for Shakespeare's time because then patriarchalism was a viable political theory; its basic concepts form part of the thought about kingship published by James I, writers employed by him, and other political theorists from Bodin to Filmer.[22] These writers provide an excellent introduction into formal patriarchal thought.

For a feminist study of patriarchy in the Renaissance we are not without resources. A group of historically oriented literary scholars has been investigating representations of power in Elizabethan and Jacobean culture for nearly a decade in such works as *The Illusion of Power, Patronage in the English Renaissance, The Power of Forms in the English Renaissance, James I and the Politics of Literature,* and in articles by Louis Adrian Montrose about Renaissance cultural codes.[23] All this fine work, done almost wholly by male scholars, has largely ignored the interests of feminist criticism and has been largely ignored by feminist critics in their turn.[24] It is time now to bridge the gap, and one purpose of this book is to introduce historical study of the patriarchy into feminist criticism. By privileging female characters and neglecting the patriarchal institutions which surround them, many feminist critics concentrate on only part of the whole representation, just as scholars interested in power often write as if Elizabeth were the only woman in her England. Those of us who are feminist critics should begin to deal with the implications for the representations of women in the male fantasies produced by the politics of Elizabethan and Jacobean society. Investigation of some of those implications is one topic of this study.

Let us consider one example of the difference between ignoring the patriarchy and taking it seriously as historical fact. Of *Pericles, Cymbeline,* and *Winter's Tale* Linda Bamber remarks, "In Shakespearean romance the feminine is infinitely valuable, capable of being utterly lost but capable of miraculous self-renewal. Again, the nature of the feminine is congruent with the nature of the world outside the Self."[25] This is a comforting idea to the feminist, and the one I, too, held before studying the concepts and representations of seventeenth-century patriarchy. If we use political discourse and other patriarchal art to read the plot structures and language of the three romances, we discover that the mothering of the father by the daughter and the miracle of the children's rebirth are used to allow the father to absorb female generativity—for the father to give birth to his children without the mother, who in two plays is conspicuously absent during her fertile years. The first reading is commonsensical and grants power to women; the second is historically accurate and essential to know if we are to understand the many ways in which the patriarchy has maintained its control of female reproduction.

More is at stake in the historical study of patriarchy than a context for reading Shakespeare's romances, important as to that may be to Shakespeareans. Such investigations can yield knowledge about the basic and enduring features of patriarchy, as well as a sense of how those features have changed historically. That understanding of change can free us from the assumption that "'twas ever thus," that there is such a thing as *the* human condition. By knowing that Shakespeare's representations of women and patriarchy and his use of genre are all historically contingent, critics are also free from the need to co-opt him into contemporary ideas, such as the questioning of patriarchy. Instead, we can understand that Shakespeare wrote for changing audiences during his career, and as they altered, his approach, even to a given genre, modified too, and along with those alterations in subgenres came differing representations of women and patriarchy. From this perspective, then, there is never one view of women or of patriarchy that we can call Shakespeare's and so there cannot be one to identify with our own. Both he and we are historically bound, but free to change. So the purposes of this study are to establish a historical context for the changes in the representations of power relationships within three groups of comedies and to introduce a historical perspective on patriarchy into feminist criticism of Shakespeare's plays.

My argument is that Shakespeare moved from one subgenre of comedy to another to appeal to the differing audiences for which he wrote from the later 1590s to the end of his career. I see his romantic comedies among several genres[26] which appealed to Shakespeare's own generation. With its fantasy of courtship of a powerful woman and a profitable marriage, such comedy was attractive to the Elizabethans who came to maturity in the nineties. These men put enormous pressure on the courtier system of government, "the system through which the Queen and her chief ministers governed the country, and through which her courtiers sought to rise to honors, to power, and to wealth to attain those ends."[27] Increases in population and in education, the expenses of the Spanish war and Elizabeth's parsimoniousness, the growing wealth of some families and the general inflation converged to produce great demands for reward on a system which had little capacity or motivation to meet them.

Artistic genres, such as the sonnet sequence or the comedy of courtship, which presented a powerful woman who frustrated or responded to the suit of a suppliant male, were especially meaningful to this audience. In the romantic comedy, marriage to a wealthy or titled woman could suggest social advancement for the often rebellious young man, who was loved, not for his birth or achievements, but simply for being himself, for having true merit. These fantasies could also have been compensatory for audiences in a social order where one was seldom valued for one's self and few could hope to marry for love. In Shakespeare the fictions consistently deny profit motives in marriage through male prodigality and deal with anxieties about women's power and male rivalries through the theme of cuckoldry.

With the problem plays, written after James had come to the throne, all these structures changed. *All's Well* and *Measure* are part of comedic subgenres in which the father-ruler seeks to control the sexuality of his subject-children. A male is now the powerful figure, and male desire is perceived as disruptive to the social order. Marriage is no longer the fulfillment of wishes, but a means of regulating society by a monarch who enforces marriage if necessary. In the plays of enforced marriage, such as *All's Well,* the men become prodigal in their response to the constraint placed on their desire and the women preserve the relationship through suffering. Women sometimes pursue the men, seeking rights with the support of the authority, and often profit from their marriages.

The subgenres to which the problem plays belong—the drama of enforced marriage and the disguised-ruler plays— betray anxiety about the sexuality of the young on the part of authority figures. Such plays form part of a larger debate within Jacobean society, which was concerned with legal regulation of personal conduct, a controversy which arose partly from crises within ancient institutions, such as wardship, from concerns about increases in the numbers of poor and bastards, and also from convictions of the Puritan group in Parliament about controlling sinful conduct. At the personal level there is in the early seventeenth century an increasing protest against the enforcement of marriage, which may be connected to parents' anxieties about the marriage choices of their better educated, much more numerous offspring. These issues raise questions about the conduct of the patriarchal ruler, now represented as a nurturing father to his subjects: both the King of France and Duke Vincentio behave in ways which interrogate that conception of the ruler.

In the last plays—*Pericles, Cymbeline, The Winter's Tale, The Tempest*—Shakespeare represents the ruler in terms that are common in patriarchal political theory and in the art of the Stuart court to which it is engrafted. Such a development seems natural, though not inevitable, for a dramatist who was a member of the King's Servants and Grooms of the Chamber, a company which gave between twelve and twenty-two plays a year at court, among them *The Winter's Tale* and *The Tempest* in 1611.[28] The old-fashioned genre of romance provided Shakespeare with a means of mythologizing the power of the father-ruler by making it seem natural and inevitable. Here the ruler's power is expressed largely in terms of his family, the father's power being the only natural power, and so the scattering and reconstitution of the ruler's family form the basis of the action. Nobility is perceived as natural: it is easily recognized wherever it is found, and providence guides even rebellious children like Florizel and Imogen to those who preserve the succession, which is an important theme in all these plays. In the rebirth of his children the father, as we have said, absorbs female generativity, while wives are kept invisible during their childbearing years. Sexuality is a cause of anxiety, but carefully controlled in naturally chaste children. By changing the definition of nature and the role of the ruler in *The Tempest*, Shakespeare allows the reader to interrogate the mythology of the earlier romances and to see how claims of absolute power to *be*, not just be favored by, providence, are illusions of art. Reading back from *The Tempest,* then, one discovers why the earlier romances insist on their status as works of art, for they are implicitly making the same point that is made explicit in *The Tempest:* absolute power exists as an artistically contrived illusion.

It is not enough, then, to say that Shakespeare's plays, even his innocent romances, are patriarchal. We can define with some precision how they are patriarchal and how they also interrogate their representations of power. This study traces the profound changes in the representations of power in Shakespeare's comedy as he moves from one comedic sub-genre to another during his career. The changes radically transform the role of women, the nature of marriage, and filial relationships. Marriage, for example, is the fullfillment of desire in the comedies of courtship, a contractual means of regulation in the problem plays, and a necessity for the succession in the romances. Heroines move from being magnetic objects of desire to temptresses of a consuming sexuality or wives enforcing rights to daughters who mother their parents and chastely marry within rank.

Understanding these changes in their historical context is necessary, even if disquieting for the feminist reader like myself. The fact that the most attractive representations of women—those in the romantic comedies and the romances—are part of fantasies which extend male profit and power is a disturbing thought. And yet it explains why Shakespeare's wonderful heroines and miraculous daughters had as little effect on the general lot of women as Elizabeth's long and brilliant reign.[29] While the queen could manipulate male ideologies of power to maintain herself, the same rhetoric could reverse the process and control the images of women for its purposes. I also find it painful to understand that the drama of enforced marriage is a structure which represents the male as reconciled to constraint on his desire by the patriarchy through his wife's suffering, and it can be even more disturbing to discover that by Shakespeare's time Griselda's suffering masked a marriage for the wife's profit. Disquieting, too, is the realization that the two comedies in which women enjoy the support of the ruler—*All's Well* and *Measure*—are called problem plays in part because women are given the resources to pursue their rights. Yet, however disturbing these insights may be to me as a modern feminist, they are a means of knowing the roots of the predicament of women today and also an explanation of why Shakespeare's plays may seem protofeminist and yet be patriarchal to the core.

CHAPTER ONE

The Comedies of Courtship: Men's Profit, Women's Power

Shakespeare's middle comedies, *As You Like It, The Merchant of Venice,* and *Twelfth Night* present the courtship and marriage of a socially superior woman and a relatively impecunious man, a fantasy which would have been deeply appealing to Shakespeare's own generation, especially while Elizabeth I ruled England. *Much Ado about Nothing* presents a variation on the pattern, as does *Love's Labour's Lost.* The marriage, which usually represents monetary profit or social advancement for the men, means subordination for the women, who may have been spirited and powerful during the courtship. But the *de facto* conjugal relationships will not be that simple, and Shakespeare suggests their complexity through a combination of jokes about cuckoldry and the wife's forgiveness of the husband's errant behavior. By modulating these themes and varying the combination of ingredients, Shakespeare defines the character of the various marriage relationships.

25

Love's Labour's Lost, a comedy of the early period that contains all these elements, can provide a paradigm by which to read the middle comedies and relate the structures of courtship and marriage to the theme of cuckoldry and the gesture of forgiveness. We recall that the Princess of France and her attendants visit the King of Navarre "on serious business," to negotiate repayment of war debts and the fate of Acquitaine, a circumstance which, like her father's death at the end, calls attention to her public station. Her demeanor is also more dignified than that of the youthful King who, as Boyet observes, falls instantly in love with her. The men's behavior is silly enough that the women not only mock the men's original vows and pretentions, but also set the terms upon which each "world-without-end bargin" may be made. The courtly relationship gives the women control over the suppliant men, and Shakespeare accents this power by making the men confused about their values. Thus, as the Princess says, their loves were taken "like a merriment." The King asks the pardon of the Princess for the ridiculousness of his behavior: "Now, at the latest minute of the hour, / Grant us our loves" (5.2.797–98).[1] But the Princess refuses until he proves his constancy by remaining true to his offer for the year of her mourning.

As soon as he observes the lords begin to woo the ladies, Boyet, who watches the antics with detached understanding, begins talk of horns and Queen Guinover of Great Britain (4.1.110ff.). From this point on, the cuckold image is carried through subsequent scenes by chatter about deer, the pricket the Princess killed, the King's hunt, and Berowne as a sheep. At the end of the scene in which the ladies mock the Moscovites, Katherine teases Longaville in the same terms:

> *Long.* Look, how you butt yourself in these sharp mocks!
>   Will you give horns, chaste lady? do not so.
> *Kath.* Then die a calf, before your horns do grow.
> *Long.* One word in private with you, ere I die.
> *Kath.* Bleat softly then; the butcher hears you cry.
>   (5.2.251–55)

So we are prepared for the burden of Spring's song at the
end, even though the marriages are a year away:

> The cuckoo then, on every tree,
> Mocks married men; for thus sings he,
> > Cuckoo;
>
> Cuckoo, cuckoo: O word of fear,
> Unpleasing to a married ear!
> > (5.2.908–12)

All the elements of the paradigm for the reading of the
middle comedies are here without the complexity of Shakespeare's developed art: the courtship in which women have
power and control the action, a heroine of high station,
somewhat childish or errant males, a request for forgiveness
of the man by the woman, and the cuckoldry theme before
marriage has begun. The gesture of forgiveness implies the
privilege of the males to err with impunity. The cuckoldry
theme implies the opposite for women: it represents the one
power women retain in their subordinate state and yet is
based on the double standard of patriarchal marriage, in
which the erring wife brings opprobrium on her husband.
The theme creates anxiety about the power of women and
allays it. Therefore, the strong women in *Merchant, As You
Like It,* and *Much Ado* use the theme. It is muted in *Twelfth
Night,* where women are relatively passive. In the middle
comedies all the elements of the paradigm are present, but
they are orchestrated for the distinctive effects of each play
and to define individual relationships. Let us examine the
terms of these structures, beginning wih courtship.

Courtship

The language of courtship in itself conveys power on
the woman who is wooed by the male suitor, but Shakespeare
and his contemporaries encoded the language of love so that
for them the woman was especially powerful in such a relationship. The Elizabethans inherited a courtly love language

that had been used to express and disguise social and political ambition: "Love lyrics could express figuratively the realities of suit, service, and recompense with which ambitious men were insistently concerned as well as the frustrations and disappointments experienced in socially competitive environments."[2] In France and southern Germany the desire for wealth, position, patronage had been fictionalized as wooing a socially superior woman.[3] The fiction of love could be used to express the desire and frustration of younger sons in their rivalry for a place in the social structure.[4] Thus the language could be used, as courtly language frequently was, to deny the very motives it expressed. Still, the enormous power given to the lady in this code is conveyed by the variety of metaphors in which the relationship can be written. Sometimes the lady is an oppressive landlord:

> These Eyes (thy Beauty's tenants!) pay due tears
> For occupation of mine Heart, thy Freehold,
> In tenure of Love's service! If thou behold
> With what exaction, it is held through fears;
> And yet thy Rents, extorted daily, bears.[5]

Sometimes she is a victorious enemy:

> Yet I myself a conqueror repute
> In fight continual, like victorious mart
> Yet ever yield, as ever overthrown.
> To be, still prisoner! is my suit.
> I will be, still, thy captive known!
> Such pleasing Servitude
> Viciorious Conquest is, and Fortitude.[6]

Sometimes a patron: "Your client, myself; shall Stella handle so?"[7] But she is most frequently a ruler to whom the lover is subject:

> Her state brooks not poor souls come so nigh her.
> Yet I protest my high aspiring will
> Was not to dispossess her of her right:

> Her sovereignty should have remained still,
> I only sought the bliss to have her sight.[8]

And yet the linkage to the court and its ambitions may be specifically denied, as in the following, entitled *Megliora Spero:*

> Faction that ever dwells in Court where wit excels,
> Hath set defiance.
> Fortune and Love have sworn that they were never born
> Of one alliance.
> Cupid which doth aspire to be god of Desire,
> Swears he "gives laws;
> That where his arrows hit, some joy, some sorrow it:
> Fortune no cause."[9]

Still for the Elizabethans the serious courtship of the unmarried woman who ruled them for decades was a compelling reality,[10] and so her name can be substituted for any sovereign lady love with perfect decorum:

> Blest is Arcadia's Queen! Kneel Swains, and say
> That "She (which here chief Nymph doth reign)
> May blessed live! to see th'extremest year!"
> For sacrifice, then, lambs and kidlings kill!
> And be, by them, Eliza glorified!
> The Flower of Loves, and pure Virginity!
> This Delian Nymph doth amaze![11]

We also know that the relationship was reciprocated: Elizabeth cultivated and manipulated the ambitions of her courtiers in developing a cult which eroticized political transactions.[12] As a result her officers of state wrote to her in the language of love.[13] The combination of a language already encoded and a woman as the supreme power in a hierarchical society made almost inevitable that Elizabethan fictions of love ascribe great power to the woman.

In the middle comedies Shakespeare gave a variety of kinds of power to his heroines. Portia, the most formidable, is wealthy and beautiful, a magnet for suitors from the world over. In fact, the competition for Portia's hand combines monetary language—gold and silver—with terms of merit— deserving and giving. She is intelligent, witty, and capable of dealing with complex legal and, apparently, mercantile questions. She is quite at home in male disguise, and although she is subordinated to her father's will, she proves a match for it and for all the destructive forces Venice can offer. She is in control of the action in the Venetian court and in the return to Belmont. She not only begins the jokes about cuckoldry but also intrudes into male competition with Antonio for Bassanio's loyalty. Perhaps a woman can be powerful in *Merchant* because of the importance of wealth in the play. In Venice wealth transcends or threatens social boundaries, and Portia is wealthy.

Hero is Leonato's only heir, and as such, a good match, but temperamentally she is chaste, silent, and obedient, while the powerful woman in *Much Ado* is, of course, Beatrice, whose tongue is her weapon. She is "my Lady Disdain," whose scornful attitude would match any sonnet lady's. Without a father to obey, feisty, angry for Hero, she would become a man to defend her. She expects Benedick to kill Claudio because of the injustice to her cousin.

Rosalind, in *As You Like It,* is also witty and the daughter of the rightful ruler, although he is not in power for most of the action. When banished from the court, she is fearful and depends on Celia to suggest a refuge in Arden; only then she decides to disguise herself as a man and the disguise helps her control her fears: "We'll have a swashing and a martial outside, / As many other mannish cowards have / That do outface it with their semblances" (1.3.119–24). Once in the forest Rosalind's control of the action increases, and although she momentarily regrets her disguise when she learns that Orlando is also in the forest, she quickly vows to deal with him as a "saucy lackey and under that habit play the knave with him" (3.2.312). Thus, she arrives at the marvelous androgyny about which so much has been written. She becomes Orlando's teacher, lover, friend, "half a kind of mysterious goddess of the woods who finally gives herself as a prize to her most faithful votary, and half an eager young woman, her femininity oozing out of her disguise, who behaves very much as though she believed in the Petrarchan sentiments she mocks."[14] She sees her forest courtship as rivalling her father's exiled court. Having weathered Orlando's injury, Rosalind arranges the conclusion of the action: "Believe then, if you please, that I can do strange things: I have, since I was three years old, conversed with a magician, most profound in his art and not damnable" (5.2.66–69). Phebe has fallen instantly in love with her, but the disguise allows that Silvius will have his love.

It is instructive to compare Olivia and Viola of *Twelfth Night* with these energetic women, for although they have the capacity to be as strong as Rosalind or Portia, neither chooses to exercise her potential. Unlike Rosalind who grows more vigorous as she likes her disguise, Viola feels that she and Olivia are victims of hers, that Time must solve her problems. Indeed, as the action develops, she becomes more beleaguered by the males, even Sir Andrew. Even when Orsino threatens her life, she submits until he learns the truth. The play does not offer an occasion on which the patient Viola would threaten the Duke with cuckoldry.

Like Portia, Olivia is wealthy and possesses a large household, but she has chosen to withdraw from any courtship by the Duke, though she does quickly respond to Cesario's winning ways, and Sir Andrew's hopes are encouraged by Uncle Toby. Malvolio's ambition for Olivia's hand seems a parody of the legitimized ambitions of suitors in the other comedies, another denial of male ambition in these profitable marriages. The courtship of Olivia is structured so that she is never really the Petrarchan lady, for she quickly begins to pursue Cesario, and Sebastian's marriage to her is a lucky accident which he rapidly accepts, another effect which denies the profit motive. With relief he views her management of her large household as evidence that she is not insane. *Twelfth Night* seems to represent parodic versions of several structures in the middle comedies, as if Shakespeare had worked the vein and prepared to move into new sub-genres.

Errant Males

If we return to our paradigm in *Love's Labour's Lost* we remember that the King of Navarre and his circle are ridiculed for their self-engrossed vows to withdraw from life to art, as well as for their awkward effort to conduct a courtship, once they have admitted their feelings toward the ladies. In their misgovernment the King, Berowne, Dumaine, and Longaville are an extreme version of the males in the middle comedies. All of the males have slightly errant natures, though these express themselves in a wide variety of ways, depending upon the character of the play. All have some excess, even if only of energy, as with Sebastian, and this leads them to action for which most seek forgiveness from the women. In this behavior the men of the middle comedies resemble a pattern in Elizabethan life and art described by Richard Helgerson in *The Elizabethan Prodigals*. Helgerson shows how a group of writers (Gascoigne, Lyly, Greene, Lodge, and Sidney) used the pattern of the prodigal son story to mediate a cultural conflict between the demands of civic humanism or parental expectations and their own desires to write poetry in the Italian tradition of courtly romance:

> If both civic humanism and courtly romance were to figure in a single life or a single literary work, they could not often do so as parts of a coterminous union, but rather in some dialectic of opposites, in a structure like that of the prodigal son story, with its pattern of admonition, rebellion, and guilt. I see humanism and romance as opposed members of a single consciousness, as the superego and id of Elizabethan literature, competitors in a struggle to control and define the self. Humanism represented paternal expectation, and romance, rebellious desire. Humanism provided the governing design, the beginning and the anticipation of the ends, for most Elizabethan fiction and for much Elizabethan poetry and drama as well; romance provided the impulse, a motive

for action, which carried the youthful protagonist from that beginning to that end or, on occasion, to another made in the image of desire rather than of moral expectation.[15]

Most of Shakespeare's young men are not reacting against direct parental admonitions, to be sure, but they express rebellious desire in vocabularies like those used by Lyly, Greene, and Lodge, and then they put the powerful lady in the parent's place by asking her forgiveness.

Bassanio is prodigal of his wealth, as he tells Antonio: "my chief care / Is to come fairly off from the great debts / Wherein my time something too prodigal / Hath left me gag'd" (1.1.127–30). We soon see that he is still spending on new liveries for Launcelot Gobbo. The solution to his problem is, of course, to borrow from Antonio to pursue Portia's fortune, the Golden Fleece, "which makes her seat of Belmont Colchos' strond" (1.1.171). Bassanio's extravagance fits the language of *Merchant,* where love is money,[16] while it also has the effect of denying any mercenary motive in courting Portia: we know money does not mean anything to the prodigal Bassanio, who will therefore choose the lead casket, hazarding all, just as he told Antonio he would find a lost arrow by shooting another after it: "bring your latter hazard back again / And thankfully rest debtor for the first" (1.1.148–52). His display is courtly and quite in accord with his role as suitor to a great lady. Because the prodigal pattern is encoded to convey courtly romance, Bassanio's generosity increases our sense of his stylish exuberance, and so his gesture of giving the doctor the ring Portia has given him seems quite in character, and her calling him to account for it in such an elaborate way presages a new regime in his life. As Portia extracts the plea for forgiveness, she acts as a rather heavy parent.

At the beginning of *Much Ado* Benedick rebels at the notion of Claudio's courtship of Hero because he does not trust women: "That a woman conceiv'd me, I thank her; that she brought me up, I likewise give her most humble thanks. But that I will have a rechate winded in my forehead, or hang my bugle in an invisible baldrick, all women shall pardon me. Because I will not do them the wrong to mistrust any, I will do myself the right to trust none; and the fine is, for the which I may go the finer, I will live a bachelor" (1.1.228–35). Such distrust, which is expressed in terms of cuckoldry, can easily feed a virilent misogyny, as it does for Claudio when he believes Hero unchaste. But because Benedick is tricked into trusting Beatrice, he turns with her into a rebel against his fellows, a change from which he never recovers. It is, therefore, Claudio who must express repentance to Leonato for having wronged Hero.

The gentle Orlando's rebellion in *As You Like It* is socially profound, yet its terms deny any ambition on his part. Orlando is a younger brother, with all that implies,[17] and he is not being cared for by Oliver according to their father's will. Although Orlando resents his servitude, it is Oliver's threat to his life that sends him into the Forest of Arden. There he finds a better patriarchy in the Duke Senior's pastoral court where he can be valued according to his merit. Ironically, Orlando's flight causes Duke Frederick to dispossess Oliver.

Orlando spends his time in the forest courting both the Duke Senior and Rosalind. The former courtship assures that he will be acceptable as the next heir to the realm, while the latter shows just enough excess for him to be mocked and creates just enough conflict for him to need forgiveness from his lady. Rosalind, for her part, resents the time Orlando spends with her father whom she perceives as a rival, while Celia accents the bravery and folly of Orlando's manners:

> He attends here in the forest on the Duke your
>   father.
> *Rosalind* I met the Duke yesterday and had much question
>   with him. He ask'd me of what parentage I was. I told
>   him, of as good as he; so he laugh'd and let me go. But
>   what talk we of fathers, when there is such a man as
>   Orlando?
> *Celia* O, that's a brave man! He writes brave verses, speaks
>   brave words, swears brave oaths, and breaks them
>   bravely, quite traverse, athwart the heart of his lover, as

> a puisny tilter, that spurs his horse but on one side,
> breaks his staff like a noble goose. But all's brave that
> youth mounts and folly guides.
>
> (3.4.31–43)

Because of his dual courtship, Orlando is constantly tardy in his meetings with Rosalind, and she becomes waspish with him when he must leave her to attend the Duke. She sounds more like a parent than a lover as she warns him of censure if he is late again. He is fleeing her shrewish remarks when he comes upon the female snake and the lioness "with udders all drawn dry," threatening Oliver. There may be some suggestion of rebellion against the female in slaying the lioness, as Montrose argues.[18] In any case, Orlando tires of the courtship once his brother is going to marry Celia.

Duke Orsino in *Twelfth Night* exhibits the most extreme case of courtly excess in this group of plays. He dotes on the role of lover, posturing for his followers and distant from his lady. His mind is like an opal, but he thinks women inconstant. Orsino's devotion to Olivia has become a fiction of Petrarchan self-pity, puns, and fancies. Their courtship is a parody of the others, and it cannot lead to marriage. Instead, Viola teaches him, man to man, about how men make brave vows they seldom keep and how women "are as true of heart as we" (2.4.106).

In fact, we cannot resist the conclusion that this fantastical Duke is well off married to the patient and resourceful Viola. But in the meantime, Viola's double has intruded with genuine male energy into the attentuated games of Illyria and begun to fight with Sir Toby and Sir Andrew. Olivia seems quite parental in breaking up their initial scuffle, but because the identities continue to be mistaken, Sebastian must ask Olivia's forgiveness for the drubbing he finally gives the pair. This gesture echoes more subtle ones in the other plays. In the later romantic comedies, *As You Like It* and *Twelfth Night,* Shakespeare complicates the pattern with which he began the subgenre in *Merchant* through doubling and paralleling characters and actions. Each play has a distinctive quality which gives vitality to the Petrarchan fantasy.

Marriage

As the comedies drive toward marriage, the men look forward to social advancement and the women to subordination. The impoverished Bassanio marries great wealth; Orlando, a younger son, becomes the Duke's heir; Claudio gains the only heir of the Governor of Messina; the shipwrecked Sebastian marvels at his good fortune, which he has no intention of refusing:

> This is the air; that is the glorious sun;
> This pearl she gave me, I feel't and see't;
> And though 'tis wonder that enwraps me thus,
> Yet 'tis not madness. . . .
> .   .   .   .
> For though my soul disputes well with my sense
> That this may be some error, but no madness,
> Yet doth this accident and flood of fortune
> So far exceed all instance, all discourse,
> That I am ready to distrust mine eyes
> And wrangle with my reason that persuades me
> To any other trust but that I am mad,
> Or else the lady's mad.
>
> (4.3.1–16)

Malvolio's ambition represents, as we have said, what must be denied or largely submerged in the genuine attachments, as does Sebastian's accidentally marrying great wealth. But Shakespeare's comedies do also present a fact of Elizabethan life for a lucky few: "For a young man of gentle birth, the fastest ways of moving up the social scale were the lotteries of marriage with an heiress, Court favour, and success at law. The first of the three is usually neglected or ignored by social historians, but it was probably the commonest method of upward movement for gentlemen."[19] From the sixteenth century on, a majority of the English nobility married commoners, usually gentry, to be sure.[20] Realistically, this aspiration was available to the tenth of the population who were gentry and above. Yet, the existence of even a tiny minority of such unions kept the idea alive. And the movement of wealthy yeomen into the lesser gentry was also "a well-established feature of the society."[21] An heiress to a considerable fortune could be an attractive match for an impoverished younger son of a noble family. Even if one could not aspire to such a marriage, it could be a metaphor of one's heart's desire. That is, as we have seen in the sonnets, the adored lady could be a symbol of any of life's aspirations: money, title, fame, or power.

> In the context of the powerful socioeconomic realities of Elizabethan England, including those marriage arrangements that left little room in the experience of the gentry or nobility for romantic love, amorous mutuality was a compelling cultural fantasy. It created a situation of open competition and reward through merit that served as an ideal not only for love relationships but also for other kinds of social transactions. From the time of the early Tudor interlude *Fulgens and Lucres* through Shakespeare's romantic comedies, marriage for love was a metaphor for advancement by merit rather than by birth or influence. But, given the established social order, in neither love nor politics did this system obtain. Thus the literary depiction of a love-match could compensate, but only imaginatively and emotionally, for the way things were.[22]

Such a fiction would have been especially satisfying to Shakespeare's own generation, who were more aspirant than their parents,[23] but, largely because of population increases, faced a dwindling relative number of places at court, in the state bureaucracy, or in the church.[24] The universities, then as now, were producing a surplus of educated men for a relatively small number of available positions.[25] To a group with many frustrated ambitions, the idea of great gains for simply being one's own fine self had great appeal, and the literary genres representing such fictions were significant for the 1590s.

Marriage was a particularly appropriate metaphor of establishing a man's worth because in the Elizabethan world it signified his entry into full membership within society.[26] Marriage meant establishing a new economic unit, a set of

lifelong attachments, as well as important kinship relationships: "A man might be merely the eldest in the female line
of a minor gentle family, yet end his life as a titled magnate
or even a peer. The point of present importance is the web of
kinship, to use a phrase of the anthropologists, which en-
folded every family in the ruling segment. It was not simply a
community of interest, a political or economic grouping, it
was a lineage, a clan. Entry into it was by marriage."[27]

For the woman, things were less heartening, which was
doubtless why innumerable texts taught that marriage was
the only true mission in a woman's life. Whether she was a
queen or a fishwife, a woman was subservient to the man she
married. Defending Elizabeth's right to rule in response to
John Knox, John Aylmer still argued that a woman can rule
as a magistrate and obey as a wife.[28] No matter how well
educated she might be, how intelligent or capable, she was
legally no person once she married. Only a tiny minority of
Puritan sects advocated greater equity.[29] As a consequence,
any new ideas about women's education or developments in
the concept of the gentlewoman were defeated by marriage.[30] At the end of her book-length study of the lady,
Ruth Kelso observed:

> The real obstacle to framing a consistent, complete ideal
> portrait of the lady of the renaissance lies not in whatever
> differences may be found in time, place, or religion, but, as
> has already been pointed out, in the failure of renaissance
> theorists to see the lady for the most part as other than a
> woman. It is on the rock of marriage that renaissance theory
> foundered. Almost all writers on women saw them as wives
> and could not view them in other roles, though they had no
> difficulty at all in viewing the gentleman without reference to
> his domestic role.[31]

We may be struck here with the ironic truth of Jessie Bernard's description of "his" and "her" marriages for the Elizabethans.[32] Although marriage was of supreme importance
for men and women in Shakespeare's world, the meaning of
the relationship differed greatly for the genders. An impru-

dent marriage could ruin a man's prospects, as we know from the lives of Donne and Raleigh, but men did not experience the virtual loss of individual identity experienced by women, at least legally and theoretically.

So Portia, the most aggressive and self-conscious of our heroines, is fully aware of what she gives up to Bassanio, quite as she has chafed under the terms of her father's will. She does not intend to let Bassanio forget for a moment what he will gain from her: she goes on for twenty-five lines in which she first humbles herself and then describes in detail what her husband has won in choosing the lead casket, which denies all profit:

> Myself and what is mine to you and yours
> Is now converted: but now I was the lord
> Of this fair mansion, master of my servants,
> Queen o'er myself; and even now, but now,
> This house, these servants and this same myself
> Are yours, my lord's. . . .
>
> (3.2.168–73)

Bassanio's response is to compare Portia to a great prince addressing a pleased multitude. What Portia does here is to reverse the denial, which Bassanio's choice of the caskets and prodigality have achieved for him. By saying she will be humbly subservient to her new husband, she puts him and us on notice that she will hardly give up her power in a trice, and Bassanio's image of her as ruler tells her and us that he understands her denial.[33]

Although marriage could mean the attainment of one's heart's desire for the prospective husband, the relationship also carried a new threat to his identity: becoming a cuckold. As Coppelia Kahn observes, the double standard of sexual morality extends male competition for women into marriage: "The double standard grants free sexual activity to men only, but marriage, by making their honor and virility depend on their wives' chastity, turns that sexual freedom into a threat. It makes every husband a potential cuckold, and gives every man, married or not, the opportunity to 'plume his will' by cuckolding his friend."[34] The cuckoldry jokes are a defense against this threat, as we shall see, by insisting on the bonds of all married men, their kinship in horns, and, of course, by blaming the wife rather than the lover for the disgrace brought upon her husband.

Although law, custom, sermons, and books of advice told women to be subservient, there is also considerable evidence that some Elizabethan women were actually little less lively than the stage portraits of them.[35] *The Roaring Girl* and *Arden of Feversham* were drawn from life, after all, and some foreign observers were impressed with the freedom English women enjoyed: "the women have much more liberty than perhaps in any other place," said Frederick of Wurttenburg in 1602.[36] The mere existence of significant controversy about their proper behavior is some evidence that women seemed to need constraints. "Masculine moralists preached home-keeping and domesticity precisely *because* the women of the English Renaissance was more inclined toward outrageous liberty."[37] There were descriptions of shrews taming husbands, of wives gadding about, drinking in taverns, dressing extravagantly, talking too much.[38] There were ballads commemorating wives' murders of their husbands: *Anne Wallens Lamentation, for the Murthering of her husband* (1616), *The unnatural Wife* (1628), *A warning for all desperate Women* (1628), and *A warning for wives* (1629). The ballads are admonitory, as their titles suggest, but they record actual female violence.

There was also a significant transvestite movement from the 1580s on. Studying the Elizabethan church courts, F. G. Emmison says, "A sexual sidelight rarely noticed by other writers bears on the wearing of men's clothes by females of lewd or lively disposition."[39] This practice seems to have produced substantial protest only after men began to adopt women's fashions and the whole trend attracted the ire of King James and the Puritan writers, but it had been going on for years before this comment: "Since the daies of *Adam* women were neuer so Masculine; Masculine in their genders and whole generations, from the Mother, to the youngest daughter; Masculine in Number, from one to multitudes; Masculine in Case, even from head to the foot; Masculine in Moode, from bold speech, to impudent action; and Masculine in Tense: for (without redress) they were, are, and will be still most Masculine, most mankinde, and most monstrous."[40] From the long endurance of this movement and from the quantity of other evidence, we may surmise that the male disguises of Shakespeare's plays, Beatrice's wish to be a man, or Rosalind's shrewish lines to Orlando probably accord as well with women's behavior in Shakespeare's own world as do the men's profitable matches. So we may conclude that although theoretically and legally a Portia or Olivia would lose in marriage the power attributed to her in courtship, a spirited wife might also be expected to retain some *de facto* power in relation to her husband. This prospect Shakespeare suggests through the theme of cuckoldry, which depends on the one power a married woman has in relation to her husband. The multiple themes of the cuckoldry tradition readily convey the attitudes of both men and women toward the marriage relationship. The themes may be modulated to contain unruliness, or may allow the unruliness to interrogate or subvert the social structures.

Cuckoldry

Cuckoldry was a very old tradition when Shakespeare and his contemporaries used it.[41] The theme formed the basis of countless fabliaux, novelle, and dramas inherited from the French and Italian writers of the fourteenth and fifteenth centuries, although it also figured earlier in the English popular tradition. The cuckold is simply a husband whose wife is unfaithful, and he is always the object of ridicule. Cuckoldry has a stable language. Its emblems are well known: the horn, which the cuckold wears, and the cuckoo, whose song forms the refrain for many on the theme, as in *Love's Labour's Lost*. Kahn has recently shown how cuckoldry depends on three assumptions: "First, misogyny, in particular the belief that all women are lustful and fickle; second, the double standard, by which man's infidelity is tolerated, while woman's is an inexcusable fault; and third, patriarchal marriage, which makes a husband's honor depend on his wife's chastity."[42] Kahn adds that patriarchal marriage, in which a wife is her husband's property, explains the disproportion of treatment between the mere disapproval of the lover and the scorn visited upon the husband. Although cuckoldry has a definite vocabulary and syntax, like many popular traditions, its meaning can vary according to context. Because Kahn is dealing with male identity, largely in Shakespeare's tragedies, she emphasizes the male side of the tradition. To understand the wives in cuckold jokes in relation to the women in the comedies, another strand of the same tradition is available, as in the following example from a jest book of 1609:

> A W * * * * *Rampant* made her husband a Cuckold *Dormant,* with a front *Cressant,* surprized by the watch *Guardant,* brought to the Justice *Passant,* with her play-fellow *Pendant,* after a coursie *Couchant.* The Justice told her that her offence was haynous in breaking the bonds of matrimony in that adulterate manner, and that she should consider that her husband was her *Head.* Good sir, quoth she, I did ever acknowledge him so, and I hope it is no such great fault in me, for I was but trimming, dressing, or ad-horning my *Head.*[43]

The vocabulary of the joke always includes a husband who is the ridiculous victim of the erring wife and her blameless—frequently nameless—lover. The joke makes certain misogynous assumptions, which Kahn accents: the wife is a whore; she is sexually insatiable (rampant and the lover is pendant); and she, not the lover, has committed the heinous crime against marriage. Then the consequences of those assumptions are violated to produce the joke. The wife fits the misogynous stereotype, but uses escape wit to pretend conformity. Surely part of the fun in *Merry Wives* is watching the clever wives trick the supreme escape artist, Falstaff, in order to remain chaste. The effect is a trick on the premises of the jokes.

Although the cuckoldry jokes assume that husbands are supposed to dominate their wives, the jokes depend on the fact that the men will fail, that the wives prove that they are not the property of their husbands, but brighter and more resourceful than their mates, who are frequently old and almost never quick of wit. The jokes play against the double standard, to be sure, but the wife is almost never punished for her adultery, and usually admired for her cleverness. The wife's sexual appetite is often a joke on the lover.[44] Although the pretext of the stories is to exhort husbands to control their wives, the effect is usually to show that they cannot, as in *Merry Wives*. At the end of Nahum Tate's *Cuckolds-Haven* (1685), the wives argue for Christian liberty: "All Reason in the World for it; and besides, Gentlemen, it is in your interest; for as you came to be Cuckolds by locking your Wives up: for ought I know, you may be uncuckolded by giving them freedom."[45] In *Eastward Ho!* (1604), the source for Tate's farce, the usurer, Security, is told that if he has been cuckolded, it proves he has a beautiful wife.[46] The clear implication is that though wives are possessions of their husbands, they will escape being treated as property by trickery.

These clever but disruptive wives may be related to the traditions described by Natalie Z. Davis in "Women on Top," where she explores patterns and traditions in images of unruly women in preindustrial Europe. In fact, Davis uses a cuckolding wife as a prime example of women who use trickery to rule a man: she is "the clever and powerful wife of the *Quinze joies de mariage*—cuckolding her husband and foiling his every effort to find her out, wheedling fancy clothes out of him, beating him up, and finally locking him in his room."[47] We may remember that *Quinze joies de mariage* was translated into English, possibly by Dekker, as *The Batchelars Banquet* in 1603.[48] Another such English figure is the protagonist of *XII Mery Jests of the Wyddow Edyth* (1573), who deceives one man after another for profit.[49] "The point of such portraits," concludes Davis, "is that they are funny and amoral: the women are full of life and energy, and they win much of the time; they stay on top of their fortune with as much success as Machiavelli might have expected from the Prince of his political tract."[50]

In everyday life the Elizabethans used accusations of cuckoldry for disruptive purposes similar to those Davis describes: harassing their neighbors or making trouble within a village. Because the actual offense of adultery was awarded only a warning and a possible sentence of penance in the Bawdy Court, the accusation of adultery seems to have been frequently made, sometimes in slander or libel and sometimes successfully.[51] Having become detached from what it signified, the accusation apparently served a variety of purposes far removed from adultery. In one case it was part of a campaign to drive a "papist" cleric from town; in another, it was part of an elaborate revenge, complete with a long ballad.[52] It seems to have been a convenient name to use when angered, without any knowledge of the individual, as in Italian traffic jams to this day. "Thus, in Elizabethan Essex, unfaithful wives' affairs gave rise to horseplay,"[53] and both men and women frequently hung horns on their neighbors' doors, fences, privies, or church seats. There are records of jeering crowds, of singing in the streets, of juvenile gangs, all mocking neighbors accused of adultery. But the main effort of the court was to keep the peace, not to enforce morality. The church courts could only mete out penance in any case. Although an occasional cuckold beat his accused wife,[54] most sought to control the Iagos of their world in the courts.

In these jokes the cuckold could behave in several ways: he could be sublimely ignorant of the affair, either because of his stupidity or the lover's cleverness. Sometimes the cuckold is told exactly what has occurred and does not understand;[55] sometimes he is lied to outrageously and accepts the lies.[56] If he suspects his wife, his attempts to control her usually backfire. If he knows about the infidelity, he may take revenge, which will frequently reverse upon him without harming wife or lover. Or he may accept the situation and become a wittol, like Allwit in *The Chaste Maid in Cheapside*, or as Touchstone suggests to Security in *Eastward Ho!* The latter work alludes to a landing on the Thames, called Cuckold's Haven, which is described by a foreign visitor: "Upon taking the air down the river (from London), on the left hand lies Ratcliffe, a considerable suburb. On the opposite shore is fixed a long pole, with ram's horns upon it, the intention of which was vulgarly said to be a reflection upon wilful and contented cuckolds."[57] When the cuckold adopts the contented and passive role of wittol, the collapse of sexual differences threatens. The tradition meets this danger as it meets the rivalry of men for women: by asserting that all married men are united as potential cuckolds. They are not in conflict with one another at all, but bonded by their common fate. This idea frequently allays male anxiety about marriage in Shakespeare's comedies.

We are now prepared to understand the complex code on which Shakespeare was drawing in *Merchant, As You Like It,* and *Much Ado.* Natalie Davis uses *As You Like It* to illustrate one of the patterns she describes in "Women on Top": a comedy which allows a woman a temporary period of dominion over the male, "which is ended only after she has said or done something to undermine authority or denounce its abuse."[58] Rosalind's disguise, her holiday humor, her claims to magic power, all relate her stay in the forest to festivals and rituals which give topsy-turvy power to women. At first Rosalind simply uses the cuckoldry theme to express her irritation with Orlando. When he is tardy, she says she would be wooed by a snail who brings his horns with him, "which such as you are fain to be beholding to your wives for. But he comes arm'd in his fortune and prevents the slander of his wife" (4.1.56–58). Although Orlando protests about Rosalind's virtue and his love, she continues to be testy throughout this scene until she envisions Orlando seeking his wife's wit in his neighbor's bed. As she becomes more saucy, Rosalind links women's intelligence with their infidelity and spells out the futility of deeming one's wife as property:

"Make doors upon a woman's wit, and it will out at the casement; shut that, and 'twill out at the key-hole; stop that, 'twill fly with the smoke out at the chimney" (4.1.154–57). Thus Rosalind makes one of the familiar points of the jokes: treating a wife as property is useless because patriarchal marriage cannot confine a clever woman.

Lest Rosalind's assertiveness and criticism of marriage arouse male anxiety, Shakespeare immediately draws on a balancing strain in the cuckoldry tradition, which is picked up in the next scene by the foresters' song during the stag hunt:

> Take thou no scorn to wear the horn;
> It was a crest ere thou wast born:
> Thy father's father wore it,
> And thy father bore it:
> The horn, the horn, the lusty horn
> Is not a thing to laugh to scorn.
> (4.2.14–19)

Potential opprobrium for the cuckold is here compensated by the kinship of all married men, which can deny a loss of male identity. This reaction to the prospect of horns has already been ventured by Touchstone as he thinks about marriage to Audrey and contemplates earning his horns thereby. In a bit of choplogic, he sees the state of married men as more venerable and honorable than bachelorhood:

> As horns are odious, they are necessary. It is said, 'many a man knows no end of his goods:' many a man knows no end of them. Well, that is the dowry of his wife; 'tis none of his own getting. Horns? Even so. Poor men alone? No, no; the noblest deer hath them as huge as the rascal. Is the single man therefore blessed? No: as a walled town is more worthier than a village, so is the forehead of a married man more honourable than the bare brow of a bachelor; and by how much defence is better than no skill, by so much is a horn more precious than to want.
> (3.3.51–64)

That Touchstone is much smarter than Audrey may lead to his complacency here, but the general tone of the play allays male anxiety through the prospect of bonding. The motifs which deal with male anxiety in the tradition demonstrate the truth of Kahn's observation that "cuckoldry, like rape, is thus an affair between men, rather than between men and women or husbands and wives, though men blame women for betraying them."[59] Like every trickster, the clever wife is an outsider who manipulates this system.

When Rosalind doffs her disguise, the theme vanishes with it, for the play moves into a celebration of the multiple marriages, which form the social control for the sexuality frequently expressed in the forest. With her father present, Rosalind accents her shift in status from daughter to wife, both subordinate roles, as all atone together. Cuckoldry serves her rebellious wit in dealing with Orlando, but disappears once the temporary period of her dominion is over.

Kahn's insight that cuckoldry is an affair between men is valuable in understanding Shakespeare's use of the theme in *Much Ado*. As we have seen, Benedick expresses his distrust of women in terms of horns. The moment he hears Claudio speak of Hero as his future wife, Benedick begins to use images of cuckoldry: "hath not the world one man but he will wear his cap with suspicion? . . . an thou wilt needs thrust thy neck into a yoke" (1.1.198–203). Although Don Pedro predicts that Benedick too will bear the yoke, Benedick protests, "if ever the sensible Benedick bear it, pluck off the bull's horns and set them in my forehead." Here misogyny forms the basis of male bonds. Polarizing men and women, feeding a deepening hostility, this attitude forms a context in which Claudio's suspicions of Hero are credible on very flimsy evidence.

The shrewish Beatrice does not help matters by intruding into male space in appropriating the talk of horns and with them the traditional male suspicion of marriage:

> *Leonato* By my troth, niece, thou wilt never get thee a
> husband, if thou be so shrewd of thy tongue.

Antonio In faith, she's too curst.

Beatrice Too curst is more than curst: I shall lessen God's
sending that way; for it is said, "God sends a curst cow
short horns"; but to a cow too curst he sends none.

Leonato So, by being too curst, God will send you no horns.

Beatrice Just, if he send me no husband; for the which
blessing I am at him upon my knees every morning and
evening.

(2.1.20–29)

Little wonder that Benedick is somewhat fearful of the
Lady Disdain. Yet after Claudio's accusation of Hero and
after Benedick has come to trust Beatrice, her assertiveness
separates him from his male friends, still strongly allied in
misogyny. In the famous "kill Claudio" scene Beatrice continues to invade the male sphere: she points out Claudio's
flimsy evidence to Benedick ("Talk with a man out at a window! A proper saying!"), she wishes to be a man to defend
Hero because "men are only turn'd into tongue," and she
expects Benedick's new allegiance to her to replace his male
bonds. His challenge of Claudio marks that change, and
Shakespeare uses the cuckoldry theme to show that Benedick
never returns to the old male camaraderie, with its pejorative
view of marriage, after Hero's name is cleared.

At the end of the play Claudio and Don Pedro, having
done penance at the tomb of Hero, seek to reestablish the old
male circle with Benedick, who remains frowning and distant. When Don Pedro wonders what troubles Benedick,
Claudio immediately concludes that Benedick is worried
about getting married:

I think he thinks upon the savage bull.
Tush, fear not, man! We'll tip thy horns with gold,
And all Europa shall rejoice at thee,
As once Europa did at lusty Jove
When he would play the noble beast in love.

(5.4.42–46)

But instead of joining the raillery, Benedick puts Claudio
down:

> Bull Jove, sir, had an amiable low,
> And some such stronge bull leapt your father's cow
> And got a calf in that same noble feat
> Much like to you, for you have just his bleat.
>
> (47–50)

Benedick emphatically rejects Claudio with the language and attitudes that used to bind them.

In the celebrative atmosphere of the end of the play, Claudio and Don Pedro's expectations of a reconciliation seem appropriate, despite the fact that their callous attitudes seem little changed. The work of ideology may be observed here, for Beatrice and Benedick should not disrupt the smooth surface of the newly reconciled society. The pair themselves go back to their old banter, after all. So the distance Shakespeare gives Benedick from his old friends is significant. And when Don Pedro asks, "How dost thou, Benedick, the married man?" Benedick refuses to see marriage as a yoke or a joke: "Since I do propose to marry, I will think nothing to any purpose that the world can say against it." And although Claudio jests of double-dealing, Benedick is resolute in his changed attitude. He tells Don Pedro, "Prince, thou art sad. Get thee a wife. There is no staff more reverend than one tipp'd with horn." So, although Beatrice's status as Hero's double serves to contain her anger and rebellion at the status quo, Benedick's conversion to the woman's part interrogates the patriarchal conception of marriage.

The Merchant of Venice illustrates the primary pattern Davis describes: "the clever and powerful wife." Although Portia lacks the overt sexuality of the wives in the cuckoldry jokes, in other ways she is their elegant double. Portia enters into masculine space through her disguise in Venice and through control of wealth and the cuckoldry fantasy at Belmont. Like Rosalind, Portia uses a threat of cuckoldry, which is an elaborate fantasy by which she reveals to Bassanio and Antonio their debts to her, and maintains control of the action until the end of the play. In a characteristic gesture, as we have said, Bassanio has given Bellario Portia's ring in gratitude for saving Antonio: given it reluctantly because the young judge asks for the ring. Back at Belmont Portia uses the ring to draw on the tradition of cuckoldry to reveal her wonderful deeds in Venice and to torment the men. Although many of Shakespeare's audience could have known it, one does not have to know the obscene joke[60] to which some of the dialogue about the ring refers because Portia reveals the import of possessing it: the ring is a symbol for the vagina. First, she says that she will sleep with the young doctor because he has the ring: "Now, by mine honour, which is yet mine own, / I'll have that doctor for my bed-fellow" (5.1.232–33). We notice that her honor is still her own; after their marriage is consummated, it will belong to Bassanio. As Bassanio asks Portia's forgiveness and Antonio stands his surety again, Portia gives Bassanio the ring, asking *his* forgiveness because she lay with the young doctor the night before. As the young doctor, Portia takes a place among the male rivalries and accents her competition with Antonio for Bassanio's loyalty. Gratiano, who has also given up his ring, exclaims, "What, are we cuckolds ere we have deserv'd it?" (265).

Portia's presence in the male world through cuckoldry indicates her continuing control of her life—and possibly Bassanio's—in marriage. As she matches the men gesture for gesture, she is much like the wife of the cuckoldry jokes, except for her wealth and status. When Antonio intercedes for Bassanio, reminding all present of his having risked his body for his friend, Portia pretends to have given her body to the doctor who saved Antonio. Then fantasy is not good enough: the men must know that she saved Antonio's life. And even displacing Antonio in Bassanio's life is not enough either: Portia must repay those responsible for Bassanio's original loan—Antonio and Shylock's surrogates must have their fortunes assured. Through these gestures Portia emphatically wins Bassanio from Antonio and from Venice.

Because this scene—and Gratiano's final line—depend on a devil's receipe for preventing cuckoldry, we may also speculate that Portia will emulate Gratiano in keeping Bassanio safely for herself, having troubled so much to win and secure him. For his part, Bassanio is complacent: his temperament is basically indulgent, and Portia has worked so hard for him, she seems unlikely to be unfaithful. In fact, Portia seems so powerful that in Bassanio's vision of cuckoldry she would be her own playfellow: "Sweet doctor, you shall be my bedfellow. / When I am absent, then lie with my wife." Conducting her courtship according to the risks in the terms of her dead father's will may have made an indelible impression on Portia: she seems determined not to lose control of her life again.

Merchant is at once the most nearly complete and the most unusual of the middle comedies. The courtship structure is most elaborate, replete with male competition in terms that blend wealth and merit. The successful suitor of the splendid lady is most clearly prodigal, given to good Elizabethan ostentation, and the lady definitely articulates her subordination in marriage. Yet she does not mean it, and we rapidly discover that she is nearly unique in the amount of power she contrives to retain to the end of the action. This determination is signalled by the fantasies of cuckoldry and forgiveness she creates. Only she reverses the forgiveness gesture, and only *Merchant* allows a wife such power. With this grant, the play effectively subverts the ostensible subordination of Portia in her marriage. This play asserts all the codes on which it depends and subverts them at the same time.

Although Beatrice is similar to Portia temperamentally, she is the shrewish double of the socially superior Hero; she and Benedick share a subordinate action in a play which reaffirms its basic social structures. Their relationship approaches mutuality: no gesture of forgiveness is necessary, and Benedick rejects his early distrust of women along with his allegiance to Claudio and Don Pedro. Yet Beatrice and Benedick seem eccentric from the major action in which Claudio and Hero resume their old roles and attitudes just as soon as Hero's name has been cleared and a ritual repentance done. Claudio jokes about infidelity in the last moments of the play. *Much Ado* implies that patriarchal marriage with its foundations in property and hierarchy will prevail, but the attitudes of the most attractive and intelligent people in the play interrogate that institution.

The effect is happier but similar in *As You Like It*. The courtship and Rosalind's modest protest against becoming property in marriage take place in the forest interlude. Rosalind arranges the exchange of herself between father and husband. The ark-like couples marrying in the presence of Duke Senior and the masque of Hymen celebrate the containment of the sexual impulse within patriarchal marriage. The memory of Rosalind's words may linger, but they seem significant only for her relationship to Orlando, hardly for the other couples. In fulfillment of the romantic fantasy, the forest has given Orlando high station, but the return to society is conservative.

The cuckoldry theme itself works in two directions. One analysis holds that because they invert roles, the jokes reinforce the status quo. This argument shows that although the jokes may question patriarchal marriage, by taking it as a basic premise and by scorning any deviant behavior, they make it a stable assumption. The inversions allow society a safety valve for conflict in order to maintain the basic structure: "Not only cuckolds, but scolds, hen-pecked husbands, and unsuitably matched couples were subjected to charivari."[61] The laughter, according to this argument, expresses the anxieties evoked by nonconformity, but the social hierarchy is stronger for the temporary inversion. Yet one purpose of Davis's essay is to modify this widely held interpretation of women's disorderly behavior. After a broad survey of literature, ritual, and festival, on which we have already drawn, she concludes that the image of women on top does not simply support the status quo:

> I want to argue that the image of the disorderly woman did not always function to keep women in their place. On the contrary, it was a multivalent image that could operate, first, to widen behavioral options for women within and even outside marriage, and, second, to sanction riot and political disobedience for both men and women in a society that allowed

the lower orders few formal means of protest. Play with the
unruly woman is partly a chance for temporary release from
the traditional and stable hierarchy; but it is also part of the
conflict over efforts to change the basic distribution of power
within the society.[62]

Shakespeare's use of the theme of cuckoldry in the comedy
of courtship has the same complex effect as the image of the
disorderly woman. Moments of rebellion are largely contained within the artistic structures. Rosalind's protest is temporary, and Beatrice and Benedick are contained in a subplot. We must also recognize the implications of the male
fantasies in the comedies. The metaphor of marriage to a
superior lady as advancement for merit works because the
lady and her property become that of the husband. That is
the basis of cuckoldry and the fact it most frequently protests. Shakespeare records both the assumptions and the protests. *Much Ado* affirms patriarchal marriage in the main action while interrogating it, not through a woman's protest,
but through her lover's change of heart. In the most fascinating case of one who really bends the mold, Portia is so in love
that she will defeat the worlds of law and commerce for
Bassanio. Now that is a delicious male fantasy which has
served to balance the play's subversion of patriarchal marriage.

CHAPTER TWO

The Problem Plays: Social Regulation of Desire

In 1603 Shakespeare's most important audience changed with the death of the old queen and the accession of James I. By May 1603 Shakespeare's company, The Chamberlain's Men, became The King's Servants and Grooms of the Chamber. In 1604–5, the year of *Measure for Measure,* the company performed eleven times at court, and seven of the plays they presented, including *Measure,* were Shakespeare's.[1] Representations of the patriarchal ruler were natural subjects to interest the new king, who came to the throne with a theory of kingship about which he had published *The Basilicon Doron.* So *All's Well that Ends Well* and *Measure* are part of a wider discourse about patriarchal authority which flourished in the first decade of the seventeenth century. As we shall see, plays of this period frequently dealt with the relation of the father to his children, and when they represented the ruler, he was often the "nourishe-father" to his subjects, an image of kingly authority James promoted in *The Basilicon Doron*.[2] The problem plays accept this vision of the ruler and explore the questions of power that such an interpretation of the ruler-subject relationship presents. Partly because they represent the ruler as parent, the authority who makes marriages and constrains sexuality, *All's Well* and *Measure* can use sexuality and the making of marriages as the central conflict in dissecting patriarchal authority. In this they also relate to another discourse for a wider audience than king and court, one which thematizes the relation of power to sexuality—the use of power to compel or direct desire. *All's Well* and *Measure* represent this theme in two forms: the enforced marriage and the bed trick, which in *Measure* becomes a radical vision of the loss of personal autonomy to the ruler.

The problem plays and the subgenres to which they belong—the drama of enforced marriage and the disguised-ruler play—form part of a culture preoccupied with problems of sexuality and the restraint of desire by authority. Why did these themes have a particular hold on the audiences of this period? Many factors gave urgency to these concerns for parents and children after the turn of the century. Although the details of the issues will be explored throughout this chapter, an introduction may also be helpful. Then, as now, the principal means of regulating sexuality was marriage, but that institution was under particular strain from a variety of generational pressures. Explosive population increases meant that parents were greatly outnumbered by their children and anxious about maintaining control of them,[3] especially in the most critical of all actions, marriage, which was, except for the will, the last gesture of parental control. Because the whole society was wealthier, their marriages were financially more critical.[4] As the parents grew more desirous to control them, the children, better educated than their parents,[5] became more aware of their alternatives and more eager to control their own lives. Scattered protests about the enforcement of marriage in the 1580s grew to a chorus by the first decade of the seventeenth century. In 1603 people did not wake up one morning worried about these long-standing problems. Instead, the Petrarchan structures gradually lost their meaning with the death of Elizabeth and gave way to comedic fantasies that portray a male ruler coping with increasingly urgent problems involving sexuality and marriage.

On the darker side, Jacobean society faced urgent social problems which appeared to lie in unrestrained sexuality.[6] As the number of people increased, the price of food rose and the wages of the laborer fell because of a surplus in the labor force. The conditions converged to produce more poor. The number of bastards born in England doubled during the last half of the sixteenth century, and magistrates saw caring for them in local parishes as a strain on funds intended for the aged and impotent poor. Although the Poor Laws of 1597 and 1601 show an intent to cope with these problems, commentators frequently observed that local authorities were lax in enforcing the laws and that scofflaws made a mockery of justice. This impression seems to have been reinforced by the growing sense of Englishmen that their new king was really not ruling the country and that he was as liberal with pardons as with honors. The urgings of Puritan reformers that fornication be punished by death formed one response to these conditions. At the same time the Puritan element in Parliament attempted to address the same problems through legislation about personal conduct, including bills to control bastardy. Yet many parliamentarians, eager to control the sexuality of the poor, were concerned that laws aimed at them would fall instead on gentlemen, who might be harassed by whores or socially inferior justices. So they frequently defeated bills which, in an effort to constrain the poor, might threaten the rest of the social order. Other commentators feared that the hunting of sin or the partiality of magistrates would distort the even application of the law. Each law proposed, each measure debated or passed raised the fundamental question of the relation of authority to personal conduct generally, frequently to sexuality specifically. In *The History of Sexuality* Michel Foucault describes the impact of the notion of population as an economic and political problem in eighteenth-century France:

> At the heart of this economic and political problem of population was sex: it was necessary to analyze the birth rate, the age of marriage, the legitimate and illegitimate births, the precocity and frequency of sexual relations. . . . Things went from ritual lamenting over the unfruitful debauchery of the rich, bachelors, and libertines to a discourse in which the sexual conduct of the population was taken both as an object of analysis and as a target of intervention. . . .Between the state and the individual, sex became an issue, and a public issue no less; a whole web of discourses, special knowledges, analyses, and injunctions settled upon it.[7]

The reaction of seventeenth-century English people to their surplus of people was not the systematic one described by Foucault, but it nonetheless gave rise to attempts by authority—parental or parliamentary—to regulate the desire of the more numerous younger generation. My argument is that *All's Well* and *Measure* are part of a larger discourse that creates and addresses this crisis.

To deal with these themes of authority and sexuality Shakespeare uses identifiable subgenres. *All's Well* and *Measure* can be read along with similar plays of the time, and, because they are part of the same discourse, they gain from being read against one another. *All's Well* is a drama of enforced marriage in which the wife's patience redeems the prodigality of the husband. The structure expresses rebellion at the constraints put on male desire and then resolves the conflict through the suffering of the wife. Through the process the play reconciles the male to the regulation of his desire and rewards the female for her suffering. Part of Helena's humiliation is arranging the bed trick, but in doing so she is following Bertram's conditions for earning him. When we compare *Measure* to *All's Well*, the change in the bed trick is immense: no longer are the engineers of the trick related to the participants—its designer is the ruler enforcing an old contract of an entirely passive woman.[8] Moreover, the Duke also forces marriages, but only at the end of the play when there is no assurance of the curative process necessary to reconcile a Lucio or an Angelo to his rejected mate. In fact, this ruler tries to compel his own marriage to a declared novice in a highly ambiguous conclusion. These changes, as we shall see, are not required by the disguised-ruler subgenre. How problematic Shakespeare has made the structures of *Measure* becomes readily apparent as soon as it is read against *All's Well*. While *All's Well* reconciles the male to his marriage, it still questions patriarchal authority, but *Measure* radically interrogates patriarchal institutions. The full argument awaits detailed discussion of both plays with their subgenres. First *All's Well* as a drama of enforced marriage.

Enforced Marriage

That parents and guardians made marriages for young people in Shakespeare's England goes without saying, but *All's Well* is unique in the canon as one play in which the king forces a ward to marry in disparagement. Such a marriage represents an abuse of wardship, a sort of marriage deeply feared and much lamented by Shakespeare's contemporaries. Concern about enforced marriage had been widespread for decades, but it became acute at the turn of the century, as we have said.[9] In *Cornucopiae* (1612), Nicholas Breton sees the forcing of marriage as a departure from past custom:

> For 'tis not now as erst in elder daies,
> When marriage was contracted by affection,
> For kindred now so much the matter swaies,
> The parties have small choice in loves election;
> But many times, ere one behold the other
> An unadvised match the friends do smother
> And howsoever they two can agree,
> Their friends have woo'd, & they must married be.[10]

Writers like Dekker in *Seven Deadly Sins of London* (1606), Barnabe Rich in *Faultes Faults* (1606), and Thomas Heywood in *A Curtaine Lecture* (1637) warn against enforcement as cruel.[11] But among the most eloquent on the question were Puritan divines, for whom marriage was the crucial institution in society. In *A Good Wife Gods Gift* (1623) Thomas Gataker explains that God's providence is more special in a wife than in wealth and that love must be free: "The verie offer of enforcement turneth it oft into hatred."[12] Such sentiments are echoed by William Gouge in *Of Domestical Duties* (1622) and earlier by William Perkins in *Christian Oeconomie* (1609).[13] For Shakespeare, however, a striking formulation occurs much earlier in George Whetstone's *An Heptameron of Civill Discourses* (1582), a source for *Measure*. I quote in full because Whetstone provides several terms the dramatists develop: "I crye out uppon forcement in Marriage, as the extreamest bondage that is: for that the rausome of libertie is y death of the one or y other of the married. The father thinkes he hath a happy purchase, if he get a riche young Warde to match with his daughter. But God he knowes, and the unfortunate couple often feele, that he byeth sorrow to his Childe, slaunder to himselfe, and perchaunce, the ruine of an ancient Gentleman's house, by the riot of the sonne in Lawe, not loving his wife."[14] This statement is part of the whole second day's discourse devoted to enforced marriage, which carries the marginal gloss, "Love will not be constrained," repeated forty years later in Gataker's marriage sermon.

In his city comedies Thomas Middleton portrays the conflicts between interest and desire experienced by the generation at the turn of the century, but the outcomes are those of Terentian comedy, in which the prodigal young men and their mistresses beat the old ones at their own avaricious game.[15] The desire for money and sex are mixed, and the conflicts are generational. In the plays of enforced marriage, however, the sexual desire of the young conflicts with the parental desire for wealth, and so the plots develop in terms of money: the guardians or fathers of the forced couple repay what the prodigal husband has wasted, as we shall see. In this variation of the Terentian model the fathers are not tricked, as in Middleton, but express in monetary terms their repentance at having enforced the match.

Although his contemporaries interpret enforced marriage as a plot motivated by money, in *All's Well* Shakespeare follows his Italian sources in making the play's basic motivations sexual desire. Shakespeare also follows Boccaccio in presenting Helena as a lover who surmounts overwhelming obstacles to achieve her mate through ingenuity, as do all the central figures in the stories of the third day of *The Decameron*. In transforming the terms of the enforced marriage drama with its male prodigality and the female social gain and patient suffering into sexual terms, Shakespeare takes the artistic risks which have consigned *All's Well* to the status of a problem play. The other artistic structures, fiction or drama, usually mask the social or economic profit of the Griselda with her patience and suffering, while others control her choices. Shakespeare's Helena exceeds most audiences' sense of limits on women's assertiveness. These problems are further detailed in the section below on "Patient Wives."

Wards

As Whetstone's small narrative implies, wards were frequent victims of enforcement. Shakespeare's contemporaries were acutely aware of abuses of wardship: in 1604 and 1610 Parliament requested that James abolish the Court of Wards,[16] which was eventually ended in 1646. Its survival despite enormous unpopularity and corruption depended largely on its being one of the few independent sources of revenue for the crown. A feudal institution, wardship was founded on the right of the king to service from a tenant of his land. If a tenant who held any part of his land by knight service died with minor heirs, the king possessed wardship of the land (to hire substitute service) and the heirs. He could control the upbringing of the heirs and make their marriages, to ensure that they did not marry persona ingrata. For centuries sale of these rights provided major income for the crown and landed aristocracy who enjoyed the same rights with regard to their tenants. The Court of Wards,[17] established in 1540 to deal with problems of disposing of church lands, became the focus of much corruption during Elizabethan and Stuart times.

The reason that wardship is so closely linked to enforced marriage should be clear from the following description:

> Not only the wardship of the minor holding by knight service, but also his marriage, was within his overlord's jurisdiction; and where any part of the lands inherited was held in chief of the crown, the king's right to the marriage was paramount over the claims of those lords of whom the rest was held. So it came about that the crown was able to accompany grant of wardship by grant of marriage; and indeed, from the purchaser's point of view, it was the latter, with the prospect it offered of providing for daughters or other dependents, that proved so infinitely attractive. It was the sale of marriages, however, that constituted the most spectacular evil of the whole system administered by the Court of Wards.[18]

Thus wardship amounted to a system of forced marriages unless the wards paid heavy fines to obtain freedom of choice. The only restriction on the crown or guardian in arranging the ward's marriage was medieval legislation against disparagement: a ward could not be married beneath his or her rank and could sue if the guardian attempted such a match.[19] King James advises his son Henry about the importance of a first marriage, especially that it should not disparage a man; we should recall that the king or guardian made only the first marriage of a ward:[20] "Remember also that Mariage is one of the greatest actions a man doeth in all his time, especially in taking of his first Wife: and if hee Marie first basely beneath his ranke, he will ever be the lesse accounted of thereafter."[21]

Why the landowning classes tolerated such a custom for centuries is beyond our scope here, but we do need to understand that concern had been building about wardship before the request to the new king in 1604. In *De Republica Anglorum* (1583) Sir Thomas Smith says,

> Many men doe esteeme this wardship by knightes service verie unreasonable and unjust, and contrarie to nature, that a Freeman and Gentleman should be bought and solde like an horse or an oxe, and so change gardians as masters and lordes: at whose governement not onely his bodie but his landes and his houses should be, to be wasted and spent without accounts, and then to marie at the will of him, who is his naturall Lorde, or his will who hath bought him, to such as he like not peradventure, or else to pay so great a ransome. This is the occasion they say, why many gentlemen be so evil brought up touching vertue and learning, and but onely in deintinesse and pleasure: and why they be maried very young and before they bee wise, and many times do not greatly love their wives.[22]

What seems to have intensified resentment of the Court of Wards toward the turn of the century was a great increase in the number of wardships and marriages sold. During the sixteenth century there was an increase of thirty-one times in the number of sales, and under James the average seems to have been about twice that under Elizabeth.[23]

When *All's Well* opens, Bertram is a ward of the King, "evermore in subjection." His mother expresses the well-known distress of the widow, who is bereft first of her husband and then has her child taken from her as a ward. When he arrives at court, Bertram resists being told he is too young to go to war. Thus his resentments and subjection are well established when the King forces him to marry Helena. In doing so the King makes Bertram a clear victim of disparagement. He, a nobleman, is forced to marry a physician's daughter he perceives as a servant in his mother's household. Helena, for her part, is ambitious both sexually and socially. In her revealing conversation with Parolles, Helena says she is not only eager for a sexual relationship, but that she would lose her virginity to her choosing. Parolles's response to her admission of desire is a stock expression of mutuality in marriage: "Get thee a good husband, and use him as he uses thee" (1.1.229–30). Helena does exactly as Parolles suggests, to the lasting consternation of her critics.

Bertram's resistance to marrying Helena is more than social snobbery. He has been deprived of his one right as a ward, and because Helena was raised in his mother's house and is much beloved by her, Bertram can also feel some incestuous inhibitions in a sexual relationship with Helena. She certainly expresses a similar anxiety to the Countess. The King, moreover, springs the proposal on Bertram, and then making it a point of honor, enforces the wedding with deep anger and over Helena's offer to withdraw the request. There seems every reason to read *All's Well* along with other plays of enforced marriage.

Dramatic Patterns

There is an abundant dramatic literature which deals with enforced marriage in theme, plot, or allusion. Many plays deal with the theme as a motive, device, or subplot: *Wily Beguiled* (1606), *The Maid's Tragedy* (1608), *The Atheist's Tragedy* (1611), *A Woman Is a Weathercock* (1612), *The Knight of the Burning Pestle* (1613), *Women Beware Women* (1621), *The Broken Heart* (1633), and *The Witch of Edmonton* (1658). The plays related to *All's Well* are those which use enforced marriage as the central plot and are written about the same time: *The London Prodigal* (1604), *The Miseries of Enforced Marriage* (1605), *The Yorkshire Tragedy* (1607), *How a Man May Choose a Good Wife from a Bad* (1604–5), and *The Honest Whore* (1604–5).[24] The dramas and narratives of Patient Griselda show similar features, probably because her husband feels compelled to the marriage. These works establish a definite pattern, of which Whetstone's statement provides the essential terms. After the enforced marriage the husband leaves the wife and becomes a prodigal, wasting the family substance so that his siblings and wife and children suffer terrible economic deprivation. The husband may also try to murder his wife (*How a Man May Choose* and *London Prodigal*) or murder his children and try to kill his wife (*Yorkshire Tragedy*). Yet, faced with these hideous consequences, wives in these plays remain as faithful and patient as Griselda (whose husband views himself as constrained to marry against his will), and they always convert their husbands at the end of the play. If the husband has tried to kill her, the wife's proof that she is still alive saves the husband's life and converts him. Once he is saved, those who enforced the marriage reward the couple with the money to replace what the husband has wasted, a balance for the fact that the marriage was originally compelled for greed. Through these plays there is a keen sense of marriage as an economic and social institution rather than an intimate relationship, and yet the couple is estranged because of the husband's unwillingness to love where he has not chosen. The husband's prodigality implies that male desire cannot be forced by the patriarchy. We will return to the patient wives after dealing with their prodigal husbands.

Prodigality

As we have already seen, prodigality was both a cultural code and a life script for the Elizabethans.[25] It is interesting to notice how the vocabulary of prodigality alters when it is imported into the plays of enforced marriage after its appearance in a play like *The Merchant of Venice*. Bassanio's prodigality is an expression of his courtliness and romantic bravery. His extravagance denies its need for Portia's wealth as the leaden casket denies marriage for money. In the plays of enforced marriage the husband's prodigality expresses his rebellion at the world of property, which has bought and sold him like chattel. He wastes that for which his freedom has been sacrificed, but his life is ultimately saved by his faithful wife and his wealth restored by his repentant elders. This pattern reverses that of the prodigal tradition in early Tudor drama, where, as Helgerson says, "The prodigality of a son who defies his father's counsel is ruinous, not momentarily, in the third act of a play that will surely end happily, but forever."[26] Even when they are not disastrous for

the prodigal, the early plays always represent a triumph for
the elder generation and their values. Lusty Juventus is rescued at the last minute by Good Counsel, repents and so is
saved by God's Merciful Promises.[27] In *The Disobedient Child*
the son who marries an incontinent wife against his father's
will is taken home briefly when he repents but then sent back
to the wife. The audience is told: "By your loving parents
always be ruled, / Or else be well assured of such a fall, / As
unto this young man worthily chanced."[28] The plays of enforced marriage, as we have seen, follow the Terentian
model of the triumph of youth.

By deserting Helena, Bertram is following the prodigal
pattern, although Shakespeare makes the terms of his rebellion sophisticated. Bertram's rejection of the patriarchy is
thoroughgoing: he leaves the court for the wars, having been
forbidden to go; he refuses to return to his family home or to
France while his wife is alive; he gives away his family ring;
he is disowned by his mother; and he tries to be unfaithful to
his wife. He incurs "the everlasting displeasure of the King,"
and his fellow soldiers understand his behavior for the rebellion it is:

> *Second Lord* He hath perverted a young gentlewoman here in
>   Florence, of a most chaste renown, and this night he
>   fleshes his will in the spoil of her honor. He hath given
>   her his monumental ring, and thinks himself made in
>   the unchaste composition.
> *First Lord* Now, God delay our rebellion! As we are ourselves,
>   what things are we!
> *Second Lord* Merely our own traitors. And as in the common
>   course of all treasons we still see them reveal themselves,
>   till they attain to their abhorr'd ends, so he that in this
>   action contrives against his own nobility in his proper
>   stream o'erflows himself.
>
>   (4.3.13–24)

In Parolles Bertram has a mirror figure to show him the
consequences of inconstancy to other males and to help him
mature thereby. The image of the drum, which lies at the

center of the action involving Parolles, conveys the empty values espoused by both Bertram and his follower, who is exposed by Bertram's colleagues in arms. The scapegoating of Parolles contributes to the resolution of Bertram's prodigality.

But Bertram's cynical and exploitive sexual morality, which distresses his fellow soldiers, is necessary if Helena's bed trick is to work. Helena's deception aside, the bed tricks in both *All's Well* and *Measure* are disturbing because they suggest "no difference," that to the desiring male in bed in the dark one woman is no different from another. Yet, paradoxically such must be Bertram's attitude if he is to come to love what he loathes. That Helena accepts him for what he is, that like Mariana she wants no better man, forms a social or affective balance for the fact that Helena, not the King alone, has been responsible for the enforced marriage. In Painter, the King "incontinently" promised Giletta a husband of her choice, but when she chose Beltramo, "the king was very loth to graunt him unto her."[29] Although Shakespeare softens Helena's assertiveness by having her desist when Bertram protests and having the King angrily make the marriage a question of his honor, the audience and Bertram cannot forget "that man should be at woman's command, and yet no hurt done!" Because Bertram's negative behavior is regarded as a rebellion against his marriage, the play assumes that his conduct is temporary, a state from which he will recover. This sense is important in our accepting his change at the end of the action. We know that all is to end well.

Patient Wives

In the earlier prodigal plays women are the corruptors of the youths, the reverse of their role in the plays of enforced marriage. In *Misogonus,* for example, the prodigal is primarily tempted by women:

Through wanton education he began to be contemptuous,
And sticked not with taunting terms his father to miscall;

And straightway, in lascivious lust, he waxed so licentious
That's father he did often vex, and brought him to great
    thrall.[30]

Misogonus's punishment is to have his long-lost elder brother recovered and so the play ends with him repentant but
with a smaller share of his father's wealth. Helgerson detects
a distinctly antifeminist tinge in the Tudor dramas: "women
appear in prodigal son plays only as vicious harlots, shrewish
wives, or criminally indulgent mothers."[31] In the Jacobean
plays, this changes: the wife is not a temptress, and, moreover, she redeems her husband and saves her marriage, all
through patience.

The woman's lot in these plays is not so bleak as first it
may seem, *if* she is the legal wife. If she is the man's object of
desire, like Clare in *The Miseries*, Aspatia in *The Maid's Tragedy*, or Penthea in *The Broken Heart*, she perishes out of
fidelity to that relationship. If she is the wife put through the
testing and suffering of a Griselda, and she bears all with
patience and loyalty, she gains economic and social status. By
the seventeenth-century Griselda's story in drama and fiction
had become an example of how a country girl might get
ahead in the world, as the subtitle of a romance version tells
the reader: *The Ancient True and Admirable History of Patient
Grisel, a Poore Mans Daughter in France: Showing How Maides,
By Her Example, in Their Good Behaviour May Marrie Rich Husbands; And Likewise Wives By Their Patience and Obedience May
Gaine Much Gloire* (1619).[32] The narrative, like *Patient Grissel*
(1603) of Dekker, Chettle, and Haughton, clearly illustrates
that Grisel earns her high place in society as the admired wife
of a marquis. We may also remember that in Boccaccio's
version of Patient Griselda the Marquess does not want to
marry but is persuaded by his vassals' prayers. He tells them
he is angry "to have at your entreaty taken a wife against
mine own will."[33] Griselda's trials seem to follow from the
constraint of his will and the difference in their social status.

The literal payoffs at the end of *Miseries* and *London
Prodigal* are similar economic gains for the family as a result

of the wives' constancy. In *The Honest Whore* after the Duke forces Matheo to marry the reformed Bellafront, Matheo goes through the same phase of prodigality, and Bellafront earns her reformed status in society by remaining faithful and forgiving to her original seducer. The point is that the suffering of the women and their patient fidelity is not simply exemplary, but socially and economically profitable. This practical and institutional notion of marriage may be more difficult for modern audiences to accept than the sexual implications of the bed trick. Yet the profit motives in both the enforced marriage and the role of the patient wife are encoded in the subgenre, even though the patient wives never display crass motives. The payoff is part of the structure.

In converting this pattern from economic to sexual terms, Shakespeare reverts to the early Tudor pattern: the prodigal is tempted by a woman. Therefore, Shakespeare splits the female figure into Diana and Helena and also makes Bertram the aggressor in relation to Diana. Moreover, although he retains the social discrepancy which results in Bertram's disparagement, Shakespeare also retains Boccaccio's theme for the third day, which deals with objects of desire obtained or recovered through diligence, where all objects are sexual and most are attained through trickery. Diana serves Bertram's prodigality, but at the command of Helena. Diana is the old temptress of the Tudor plays in the service of the new structure.

In creating Helena, Shakespeare complicates and makes problematical the patient wife of the enforced marriage by combining her with Boccaccio's clever wench, whose motives are ambitious and overtly sexual.[34] As we have seen, Helena follows Parolles's advice: she gets a husband and uses him as he uses her. When Bertram makes a vow to her that he does not keep, she uses his sexuality to meet hers by substituting the object. He lies to her, and she deceives him about her death and his bedfellow. As the clever wench she engineers the consummation of their marriage, shows Bertram he can love her, and binds him to her with rings and progeny. As the patient wife she behaves according to his prescribed riddles, gains the love of his people, and earns a place in his family by bearing his heir.

The audience's sense of Helena's assertiveness may be increased by Shakespeare's assigning her the language of the male in a courtly situation when she says to Bertram, "Sir, I can nothing say / But that I am your most obedient servant" (2.5.72–73). Wives are obedient, to be sure, but here Helena has reversed the usual roles of courtier and lady, a gesture which ambiguously emphasizes her support from the King, while seeming to deny any power with reference to Bertram, who is made nervous by her words and more anxious to flee the court. If we have any doubts that Bertram understands Helena's code in using the word *servant,* we have only to listen to his own courtship of Diana: "I love thee / By love's own sweet constraint, and will for ever / Do thee all rights of service" (4.2.15–17). Diana's reluctance to put faith in Bertram's golden words is wise in view of his later attitude toward her.

Helena does not just want Bertram as a lover, but as a husband. Although, like Lavache, she acknowledges physical need, she would lose her virginity as she does, chastely in marriage, a relationship designed not only for husband and wife, but for progeny as well. And so in *All's Well* the bed trick is not just the consummation of a marriage, complete with a wedding ring, it is also an act of procreation.[35] Following out the suggestion from Boccaccio about Giletta's presenting Beltramo with sons, Shakespeare more subtly turns sexuality into fecundity—marriage into family—at the end of the play.

First, Shakespeare charges with family significance the ring Helena must obtain from Bertram. Beltramo's ring had a special virtue and so he never took it off. Bertram's is a family ring, bearing presumably his family crest, the symbol of his heritage. In his rebellion, Bertram gives his monumental ring to the woman he has chosen. Second, Shakespeare adds a ring, the one given to Helena by the King and by her to Bertram. This is clearly a symbol of Helena's virginity, as we understand from Diana's lines to Bertram:

> Mine honor's such a ring.
> My chastity's the jewel of our house,
> Bequeathed down from many ancestors,
> Which were the greatest obloquy i' th' world
> In me to lose. Thus your own proper wisdom
> Brings in the champion honour on my part,
> Against your vain assault.
>
> (4.2.45–51)

Bertram's possession of Helena's ring enforces his responsibility for having had sexual intercourse with her, a responsibility he would later wish to deny when confronted by Diana. By the possession of the rings, an illicit assignation which should depend on "no difference" becomes a family affair in which wedding rings establish lasting identities. These are necessary because the next generation has been conceived and must be legitimated. Thus in the final scene Shakespeare presents both aspects of the female object: Diana, the object of desire, who has been given the family ring, and Helena, the wife and future mother, who has given Bertram her ring and her virginity. In this scene one leads to the other as her "bail."

Although Shakespeare is careful to drench the end of the play with the legitimating family aspects of sexuality, it has continued to trouble readers. Diana's insistence on her riddling exposure of Bertram's gentleman's morality has irritated critics like Quiller-Couch,[36] and her attitudes reveal one of the problematic aspects of the problem comedies. With Diana, Shakespeare creates a situation he will repeat in *Measure:* women using male sexual cynicism to gain their objects of desire. Both Bertram and Angelo assume that they may use Diana and Isabella without being used in return. They have only to impugn a woman's reputation to ruin and discard her. Yet what Helena and Mariana desire is a relationship with Bertram and Angelo, and this they gain in the bed tricks. Both are substituted for the objects of desire: Diana and Isabella. Yet Helena has more assurance of love than Mariana. After Helena appears at the end and Bertram chooses her as a wife, she assures him that he has loved her: "O my good lord, when I was like this maid, / I found you wondrous kind" (5.3.310–11).

By translating the drama of enforced marriage from economic to sexual terms through the bed trick, Shakespeare exposes its problematic structure. The patient wife's suffering, often her pretended death, transforms her into a new object that the husband can desire. Her enduring commitment to him during his extended prodigality assures the husband that she desires him and not the profit she will gain by the relationship. All these elements Shakespeare includes in this version of the structure, while making overt the substitution of the wife for the chosen woman. Yet Shakespeare understands, too, that this structure provides the wife not only with profit from the relationship, but also with social power in that she is her husband's means of reconciliation with the patriarchy. So Shakespeare gives Helena the resourcefulness of Giletta, the support of the patriarchy in the King, the Countess, and Lafew, her father's medical knowledge, and the help of the Widow and Diana. Having given her such a substantial endowment, Shakespeare balances it through a series of devices: the doubling by Diana, Bertram's casualness, lying, and cynicism, and the King's angry partisanship.

The doubling of the female figure mitigates Helena's power. Helena may have won Bertram through her wits, but Diana is sexually attractive to him. The doubling avoids giving one woman social, intellectual, and sexual power, especially where her intelligence is exercised on her own behalf. Portia, who has everything, uses it all for Bassanio, as we have seen. But Helena, who is clever on her own behalf, must substitute herself for an attractive double whom her husband woos. We have observed that Bertram's sexual cynicism is necessary to the bed trick, but it nevertheless demeans his wife.

Bertram's cynicism continues past the bed trick into the final scene where it has caused audiences centuries of discomfort.[37] As Shakespeare makes the terms of the enforced marriage structure clear, the husband must be able to change objects of desire at the end if the action is to work. Moreover, his actions must be reprehensible and forgiven by the wife to earn her social gain. Having given him a sound motive (disparagement) for rejecting Helena originally, Shakespeare continues Bertram's negative behavior to balance Helena's considerable social power. The greater Helena's resources and gains, the greater the excesses she must forgive. Bertram's lies about his behavior carry into the final scene the earlier negative comments about Bertram by his fellow soldiers. The King's criticism of him mitigates the strong bond the ruler has had with Helena and prepares for her alliance with her spouse. Bertram's casualness makes sense if he is to change objects at the end, and his jingling statement to the King accents the ritualistic character of the marital reconciliation: "If she, my liege, can make me know this clearly, / I'll love her dearly, ever, ever dearly" (5.3.313–14). Diana has spoken in riddles of the rings and proposals of marriage. Helena has performed the riddles which Bertram has prescribed and labeled him as doubly won by the ring and her pregnancy. All this is a large order to accept in a trice. The scene is not for spontaneous, powerful feelings, but a ritualistic moment in which a highly structured, formulaic response is appropriate.

Even if we accept these arguments, Shakespeare seems to have strained the genre: Helena has seemed too scheming and Bertram too uncaring to audiences of many eras. In this reaction may be seen the wisdom of Shakespeare's contemporaries, who mask the wife's power by her deprivation and suffering. The King's partiality for Helena upsets the power relations in the play and increases Helena's difficulties and Bertram's resistance to their union. Shakespeare arranges the play so that although its structures are intended to reconcile males to patriarchal institutions, Bertram is never fully reconciled to the patriarchy. This feature intensifies our sense that the play is critical of the King. First, his marriage of a ward in disparagement is a tyrannical action, especially if it is done in anger. Secondly, although he pardons Bertram for his rebellion, the King becomes as deeply angry about Helena's ring as he was when he forced the marriage, and on flimsy evidence he accuses Bertram of killing Helena (5.3.115–20). He then threatens Diana with death when she will not tell how she got Helena's ring. But no sooner are Bertram and Helena united than the King will repeat the process by providing a dowry for Diana after she has chosen her husband. We hope that she is wiser for Helena's experience. By making the King's relationship to Helena slightly erotic and very partial, Shakespeare calls in question the ruler's acting as father to his subjects. If marriages of wards are an example for such conduct of regal authority, the patriarchal model is inauspicious. Moreover, parental affection, as in *Lear*, could wreak havoc with royal judiciousness, just as the King's partiality for Helena makes him violently angry here. Thus, although its structures may reconcile the male to the enforced marriage after his rebellion, the play still invites its audience to ponder the use of kingly power in regulating personal relationships. The play implies that it may be easier to assert that the king is a father to his subjects than to rule that way. Although its processes deal with the issues of desire and marriage, the questions of the misuse of patriarchal power remain.

Disguised Authority

The play of the disguised ruler represents the patriarchy in its attempts to control or at least observe sexuality, usually in the young. In some plays decadent sexuality becomes a metonymy for social corruption; in others parents disguise themselves to spy on the courtship or sex life of their children. For the purposes of this discussion I will conflate parents, rulers, and husbands as authority figures who disguise themselves. The common element is the need to observe and possibly control one's subjects' or one's children's sexuality. As Rosalind Miles suggests, the disguised-ruler subgenre was particularly alive when *Measure* was performed at court in 1604,[38] and if we examine examples of the kind, certain patterns emerge which are useful in reading *Measure*.

Several examples present fathers who pursue their children into exile or distant settings to spy on them. In Part II of *The Honest Whore* (1604–5) Orlando Friscobaldo, disguising himself as a servant, seeks out his erring child to help her in her troubled reformed life. Two plays of enforced marriage also present disguised fathers observing their children's fortunes: in *The London Prodigal* (1604) and *How a Man May Choose a Good Wife from a Bad* (1604–5) the parents who have enforced the marriage observe the husband's prodigality and the wife's patience and learn to repent the action.[39]

The other fathers are rulers: in *The Fawn* (1605)[40] the Duke of Ferrara follows his son Tiberio to Don Gonzago's court in Urbino to observe Tiberio's wooing of Dulcimel, supposedly on the father's behalf. During the process Dulcimel makes clear that she loves Tiberio, and their marriage balances the exposure of the sexual corruption of Don Gonzago's court in Cupid's Parliament at the end. In Sharpham's *The Fleire* (1606)[41] Antifront, deposed lord of Florence, follows his daughters to England to observe their lives as courtesans (they lack any means of support) and to save them when they try to poison certain unwanted friends, making possible marriages that will assure their right to Florence and his restoration to his rule. When Fleire exposes the daughters' plan to murder Ruffell and Sparke, one of the daughters utters sentiments that echo those of Angelo about Vincentio in *Measure:*

> *Flo.* You powers devine, I *know* doe plainely see,
> Heavens starrie eyes all our villanie:
> And God in Iustice murther will reveale,
> But were I now, my life for to beginne,
> Ide be an honest wife to you, wherefore forgive me deerest
>   Lord.
>
> (5.270–75)

Similarly, in Day's *Humour Out of Breath* (1608)[42] Octavio, the usurping Duke of Mantua, follows his sons to the country near Venice to supervise their wooing: "should they chance / Upon some worthless weed I'll hinder it" (2.1). Octavio also cautions his deputies to watch his daughter: "The girl is wanton; if she gad abroad / Restrain her, bound her in her chamber door; / My word's thy warrant, let her know so much" (2.1). While Octavio's sons, disguised as shepherds, are wooing the daughters of the rightful duke Antonio in the country, Antonio's son Aspero is courting Octavio's daughter Florimel in Mantua. When Antonio is reinstated by the Mantuans, the unions of the children are means of reconciling the fathers without revenge.

West-Ward Hoe (1607)[43] offers another variation on these devices. Master Justiniano separates from his wife because he is jealous and disguises himself to tempt other wives to cuckold their husbands. In a reversal of the usual pattern, he discovers that the wives are merry but honest, and the knowledge proves curative, for when his wife wants Justiniano back, they are reconciled.

Other examples combine pervasive sexual corruption with political and legal evils. *The Malcontent* (1604)[44] presents sexual machinations as both the means to power and the image of social corruption. The usurping Duke Pietro has won the dukedom by marrying the daughter of the ruler of Florence. The intriguer Mendoza uses the exposure of Pietro's cuckoldry to become his heir and then to unseat him by revealing this evil to Florence. Mendoza plans to consolidate his power through marriage to Maria, the faithful duchess of the deposed Altofronto (Malevole). At the end of the play the sexual reformations of Pietro's wife and her lover signal political reform, and Altofronto first reveals himself to his loyal wife in a masque where Mendoza is trapped by the reformed members of the court, who are now dancing with appropriate partners: the sexual order mirrors the political order. But lest the audience conclude that society is reformed beyond the court, Maquerelle, the bawd, comments on a proposal made by a courtier to a lady: "On his troth, la! Believe him not; that kind of cony-catching is as stale as Sir Oliver Anchovy's perfum'd jerkin. Promise of matrimony by a young gallant, to bring a virgin lady into a fool's paradise, make her a great woman, and then cast her off—'tis as common, as natural to a courtier, as jealousy to a citizen, gluttony to Puritan, wisdom to an alderman, pride to a tailor, or an empty hand basket to one of these sixpenny damnations. Of his troth, la! Believe him not; traps to catch polecats" (5.6.92–100). We leave the play with a sense that sexuality is a test of all virtue, a negative force in society which must be curbed, reformed, or sent outside the pale—to the suburbs. The end implies that a good ruler might order the court, but hardly cure the whole society of its sexual ills.

Middleton's *The Phoenix* (1604)[45] ends in a similar spirit. Although its canvas is somewhat broader because it deals with legal corruption as well as sexual abuses, the comedy displays a variety of sexual evils: wife selling, incest, and elegant prostitution. All of these are evaded rather than reformed, however. The Captain who sells his wife goes off to sea; the judge who would abuse his niece is deprived of his authority, while she is married to someone who will protect her. The knight who has corrupted the Jeweler's Wife goes to prison, and in a mockery of reform she resolves to sleep with no one, including her husband. Although the surface of the play's conclusion is orderly and peaceful, the convergence of the insane Tangle with other apparently repentant characters—Falso and the Jeweler's Wife, who are quite cynical about the gesture—means that the audience holds little faith that Phoenix's land will be better in the future. Instead, one has the sense that Phoenix pardons wrongdoers in some relief at not having to punish them. Neither the law nor marriage, both subjects of eulogies by Phoenix, can efficaciously restrain sexuality.

Day's *Law-tricks* (1604)[46] is similar to *The Phoenix* in combining the themes of the misuse of law and sexual abuse. The plot that gives the play its title is a variation on the theme of enforced marriage: Lurdo has just divorced the Duke's sister, the Countess, by giving false testimony about her adultery. His motive is greed: "My avarice thought she liv'd too long" (1.1). Horatio, having helped Lurdo out of love for the

Countess, tries to poison her when she spurns his suit. By pretending to die and then reappearing, the Countess saves the lives of Lurdo and Horatio and is finally reconciled to Lurdo. In the main plot the Duke pretends he has died in order to spy on his son, who he discovers only wants to go on a spending spree when he succeeds his father. In the meantime, the Duke's daughter discovers much sexual corruption while she is disguised as an elegant prostitute. This play contains much observation of sexual abuse, but no efforts for reform.

The spying on society, especially on the young, which the disguises make common to all of these plays, amply demonstrates the anxiety about sexuality, principally on the part of the older generation. The disguise allows parent or ruler or husband to behave like providence and see the "passes" of the young. But the patterns of the plays also reveal the extreme to which Shakespeare has taken the subgenre in *Measure,* for Duke Vincentio is the only disguised ruler who meddles directly in the sex lives of subjects in no way related to him. Most of our spies are fathers, as we have seen; Mendoza asks Malevole to pander for his own wife; Phoenix is himself propositioned by the Jeweler's Wife, his friend Fidelio is the son of the wife sold by the Captain, and Fidelio marries Falso's niece. Master Justiniano sets the citizens' wives up for cuckoldry in *West-Ward Hoe,* but he does not control them. In this context Duke Vincentio's bed trick is a striking and instructive departure from the other plays in that only Shakespeare seems to have abstracted from the anxieties represented in the spying the impulse of the ruler to intrude directly into the sexuality of his subjects. In some ways the step seems a small one: if the ruler could make marriages, he was surely determining sexual objects. Yet the plays of enforced marriage protest such unions, and although the plays also ultimately reconcile the participants to such marriages, the element of protest in the husband's rebellion and the parents' repentance is substantial. In *Measure,* however, the ruler forces both coupling and marriage in a structure which allows no curative process. That difference from the other plays needs to be appreciated. The crisis in thinking about society that could lead Shakespeare to such a bleak representation of the relation between sexuality and power can be understood by looking at aspects of the social order.

A Plethora of People

By the beginning of James's reign Englishmen were convinced that their island was chocked with people. Indeed, the population of England and Wales increased from approximately 3 million in 1500 to about 4.5 million in 1600,[47] and although plagues and wars made growth uneven, contemporaries could not help but notice the increase: "throughe oure longe peace and seldome sickness we are growen more populous then ever heretofore."[48] The growth strained food supplies and depressed real wages, producing much poverty and misery.[49] And then, as now, those in power blamed the victims for their suffering and especially for their getting of superfluous offspring. Too many people really meant too many poor for the society to support. In 1577 William Harrison says, after commenting about the large numbers of poor in the kingdom and those driven to colonies by a lack of room for them, that "yet the greater part, commonly having nothing to stay upon, are wilful, and thereupon do either prove idle beggars or else continue stark thieves till the gallows do eat them up, which is a lamentable case. Certes in some men's judgment these things are but trifles, and not worthy the regarding. Some also do grudge at the great increase of people in these days, thinking a necessary brood of cattle far better than a superfluous augmentation of mankind."[50] Thirty years later the problem seemed far more critical. During a debate on enclosure in 1607 a speaker noted, "if in London, a place more contagious than the country, the number of christenings doth weekly by 40 exceed the burials, and that the countries proportionally doth equal if not outgo that rate, it cannot be but that in this State, as in a full Body, there must break out yearly tumours and impostumes as did of late."[51] The increases were accompanied, as frequently happens, by a

fear of rebellion. The revolt of 1549 was still an active memory
for some. In 1609 Robert Gray argued for colonization in
Virginia because of the danger from a surplus of people:
"There is nothing more dangerous for the estate of commonwealths than when the people do increase to a greater multitude and number than may justly parallel with the largeness
of the place and country. For hereupon comes oppression and
diverse kind of wrongs, mutinies, sedition, commotion, and
rebellion, scarcity, dearth, poverty, and sundry sorts of calam-
ities, which either breed the conversion or eversion of cities
and commonwealths."[52] Similarly in 1612 the King's Surveyor
argued for enclosing forests and wastes: "It will lessen the
multiplicity of beggars which are begotten daily by reason
there is not placing sufficient for them considering that the
wastes and commons are not inhabited and the number of
people do mightily increase, the burden whereof is grown
almost insupportable."[53]

Although the Poor Laws of 1597 and 1601 were a genu-
inely humane attempt to provide for the growing number of
poor, there was a definite sense, which the surveyor expressed, that neither London nor the provinces could cope
with the wanderers who were the responsibility of no parish
under the law and many of whom invaded London to become part of the substantial underworld described by Dekker, Greene, and Nashe. In pleading for various kinds of
relief for the poor in 1587, John Howes observed,

> I praye you showe mee the reason whie and howe yt is possible
> that suche a nomber of poore as you make mencion of, and
> suche a masse of moneye as you wekely, monethly and yerely
> payed unto them, and the streates yet swarme with beggars,
> that no man can stande or staie in any churche or streate, but
> presently tenne or twelve beggars comme breathing in his face,
> many of them having theire plague sores and other contageous
> disseases running on them, wandring from man to man to seke
> relefe, which is very daungerous to all hir maiestes good sub-
> iects, and the very highe waie to infecte the whole kingdomme.[54]

Later in 1596 Edward Hext, a Justice of the Peace for Somer-
set, wrote to Burghley of the oppression of good people by the

idle, wandering poor who rob and consume what the working people produce. They are the chief cause of dearth as "they spend dobly as myche as the laborer dothe, for they lye Idlely in the ale howses daye and nyght eatinge and drynkynge excessively." When they are committed to jail, Hext told Burghley, the community simply has the expense of feeding them; their children are almost inevitably evil; and they frequently intimidate the law officers who grow afraid to punish them: "And they laughe in ther sleves att the lenyty of the lawe and the tymerousnesse of the thexecutyoners of yt."[55] By 1604 Parliament made an effort to control the desertion of families by making it a felony for parents of either sex to run from a family to another county.[56] "Wandering poor" was the name for overpopulation and the problems it presented to English society. Migrations to the colonies began in earnest in 1607.

Bastardy

The concern of Shakespeare's contemporaries about the multiplication of the poor frequently rested specifically on the getting of bastards. The rate of illegitimacy had doubled during Shakespeare's lifetime, peaking in 1604, the year of *Measure*.[57] Moreover, ample evidence of the widespread problem comes from the ecclesiastical courts and the courts of quarter sessions, which supervised the support of bastards born within their jurisdictions. Maurice Ashley notes, "In the Wiltshire records for 1578 no fewer than eighty-four bastardy cases were dealt with."[58] Historians' explanations for the tremendous increase point out two basic ingredients. There apparently had existed for years in preindustrial England a "bastardy-prone sub-society," made up of prostitutes, libertines, and the hard-core poor.[59] These were repeated offenders. Their circumstances and way of life are known to all readers of Nashe's *Christs Teares Over Ierusalem* (1593) or Dekker's *Lanthorne and Candle-Light* (1609).[60] This group contributed bastards to each generation, but little to what has been called an illegitimacy explosion at the turn of the century because they form a relative constant. The real increase, historians tell us,[61] arose from circumstances where an intended marriage by socially acceptable citizens was delayed by economic conditions. England had experienced deep economic crises from 1594 to 1598, which caused much dislocation in traditional marriage patterns. There were frequent postponements, even of marriages approved by parents, and sometimes progeny anticipated wedding vows by several years. Accounts of the village of Terling yield the following description:

> The explosion of bastardy at the turn of the sixteenth and seventeenth centuries is to be explained neither in terms of the activities of the "bastardy prone" core, nor in terms of a revolution in sexual attitudes. It related rather to a point of crisis in a growing disequilibrium between customary attitudes, expectations and sexual behaviour and deteriorating social and economic circumstances. This crisis affected not only the poor but also, briefly, a number of the children of their immediate social superiors.[62]

Yet even before this explosion, illegitimacy had attracted the attention of moralists like Philip Stubbes in *The Anatomy of Abuses* (1583): "It [whoredom] is so little feared in Ailgna, that untill every one hath two or three Bastardes a piece, they esteeme him no man (for that, they call a mans deede) insomuch as every scurvie boy of twelve, sixteen or twenty yeares of age wil make no conscience of it, to have two or three, peradventure half a dozen severall women with childe at once, and this exploite being doon, he showes them a faire pair of haeles, and away he goeth."[63] For Stubbes, male irresponsibility lay at the root of the problem of bastardy.

Because they could not so easily show the child a fair pair of heels, women suffered greatly as a result of the increases in bastardy. As the years passed, the punishments for the women became more harsh:

> Given the hostility of rate payers to "great bellied wenches," it is not surprising to find the treatment of sexual offenders becoming more severe. Before 1580 the only

punishment for offenders—at least if they were willing to support the child—was a few hours in the stocks. Then, in 1588, the Quarter Sessions rolls record the first case of an unwed mother being whipped at the cart's tail, although the strokes were to be "moderately given." After 1600 the sentences grew harsher: women were to whipped until their backs were bloody. After 1610 they were also sent to the House of Correction for a year.[64]

Because the Poor Laws made a bastard the charge of the parish in which the child was born, the harboring of unmarried pregnant women was a punishable offense.[65] Frequently women and babies or women about to give birth were driven outside a town so that the community might escape responsibility for supporting the child, as in the following account:

> The constable might resort to extreme measures to save the village charges. In December, 1605, a woman carrying a peddler's pack came with two female friends to Ardleigh in Essex and was harbored in an alehouse. The woman proved to be in travail, and when turned out of the alehouse tried desperately to rent a room. The constable, fearing that the child would be born in the village and become a future charge upon it, went out in the cold rain and carted all three women a mile out of Ardleigh, just beyond the bounds of the parish, depositing them at a farmer's barn door. The farmer demanded by what right he had brought the women to him and wished them taken back again, but the constable left the women in the barn, where the child was born that night. Seven or eight days later the mother decamped, leaving the newborn child to the mercy of the parish of Langham. The justices decided that the village of Ardleigh was to pay for the upkeep of the child.[66]

The nightmare of this threat survived into seventeenth- and eighteenth-century women's fiction. Sometimes, even if the father or his relatives took responsibility for the child, the mother was still punished, as in this account from 1598:

> *Savile. Southowrom.* Forsomuch as ther bene divers orders made in this Court for the educating of a base Child

begotten by Mathew Hemyngwey on the body of Dionis Savile, all which orders are now determyned, and for that Henry
Savile, father of the said Dionise, in respecte of his povertie
craveth further allowance untill the next Sessions for the re-
leif therof: Yt is therfore ordered that the Towneshipp of
Southowrom wher the said Child was borne shall pay iiijd.
and Richard Hemyngwey Father of the said Mathew ijd.
weekely untill the next Sessions towardes theducating of the
said Child, And that in the meane tyme the said Dionise shal-
be soundly whipped for her offence.[67]

Just as many moralists today are more concerned about
the welfare of the unborn than of the already born, so Shakespeare's contemporaries translated the social problem of bastardy into an issue of sexual promiscuity. The welfare of the
children may have been a problem for the parishes and the
constables, but sexuality was at the center of the issue for
thinkers like Stubbes. Stubbes blamed England's ills on early
marriage: ambitious parents, he said, marry their children in
swaddling clothes, and couples marry without maintenance,
putting up cottages at the end of every lane. Stubbes would
restrain marriage before twenty-four years, and, above all,
he would increase the severity of laws against bastardy and
fornication: "The occasion of begetting of manye Bastards
were soone cut of, if the punishment which either God his
lawe doth allowe, or els which good pollicy doth contribute,
were aggravated, and executed uppon the Offenders. . . . I
would wish that Man or Woman who are certenlye knowen
without all scruple or doubte, to have committed the horry-
ble fact of whordome, adulterie, incest, or fornication,
eyther . . . tast of present death or be branded."[68] It seems
clear that Shakespeare explores the consequences of this extreme attitude toward sexuality in *Measure* with disquieting
results. He represents the extreme use of state power—execution—to control sexuality, exacted by a magistrate of pu-
ritanical temper, because it dramatically presses the limits of
thinking on the question. That Shakespeare may have
wished to tie *Measure* to Puritan discourse like Stubbes's may
be suggested by Angelo's "immured garden," which Stubbes

identifies as a frequent place of assignation and which both Isabella and Mariana emphasize. Here is Stubbes:

> In the Feeldes and Suburbes of the Cities thei have Gardens, either palled, or walled round about very high, with their Harbers and Bowers fit for the purpose. And least thei might bee espied in these open places, they have their Banquetting houses with Galleries, Turrettes, and what not els therin sumpteously erected: wherein thei maie (and doubtlesse doe) many of them plaie the filthie persons. And for that their Gardens are locked, some of them have three or fower keyes a peece, whereof one they keep for themselves, the other their Paramours have to goe in before them, least happely they should be perceived, for then were all their sport dasht. Then to these Gardens thei repaire when thei list, with a basket and a boy, where thei, meeting their sweet hartes, receive their wished desires. These Gardens are exelent places, and for the purpose; for if thei can speak with their dear-lynges no where els, yet there thei maie be sure to meete them, and to receive the guerdon of their paines: thei know best what I meane.[69]

Shakespeare's Vienna

Shakespeare's representation of this social crisis is closer to the actual circumstances of English life than most of the disguised-ruler plays. Vienna, like London, is a city of widespread immorality, with suburbs full of brothels. Readers of *Christs Teares Over Ierusalem* (1593) can draw on Nash's images to understand how close one city is to another: "*London,* what are thy Suburbes but licensed Stewes. Can it be so many brothel-houses, of salary sensuality, & sixe-penny whore-dome, (the next doore to the Magistrates) should be sette up and maintained, if brybes dyd not bestirre them? I accuse none, but certainly iustice some-where is corrupted. Whole Hospitals of tenne times a day dishonested strumpets, have we cloystred together. Night and day the entrance unto them, is as free as to a Taverne. Not one of them but hath a hundred retayners."[70] Vienna, too, hosts a substantial subculture in Lucio, Kate Keepdown, and Mistress Overdone, whose brothel was served by the bawd-born Pompey and frequented by Master Rash, Caper, Three Pile, Deep-Vow, and over forty other denizens of the prison (4.3). The brothel was, Elbow tells us, "pluck'd down in the suburbs; and now she [Mistress Overdone] professes a hot-house" (2.1.65–66). When Escalus tells Pompey that prostitution will be forbidden in Vienna, Pompey exclaims, "Does your worship mean to geld and splay all the youth of the city?" (2.1.229–30). Both Pompey and Lucio know sexual corruption is so widespread that they see laws against it as depeopling the city (2.1.239–41; 3.2.167–69).

Although there are no references to the illegitimacy of Claudio's child if he should be executed, Shakespeare devotes an entire subplot to the issue of bastardy, an action he adds to his source. The first we hear of the theme is Lucio's ambiguous praise of the Duke to the Friar: "Ere he would have hang'd a man for getting a hundred bastards, he would have paid for the nursing a thousand" (3.2.113–16). This identifies the Duke as a lenient, nurturing ruler, more concerned about life than social enforcement. We soon discover a reason for Lucio's interest in bastards—he has fathered one with Kate Keepdown. Mistress Overdone has cared for it and thinks her arrest is Lucio's revenge: "My lord, this is one Lucio's information against me. Mistress Kate Keepdown was with child by him in the Duke's time; he promis'd her marriage. His child is a year and a quarter old, come Philip and Jacob. I have kept it myself; and see how he goes about to abuse me!" (3.2.193–98). It is later revealed that Lucio has appeared before the Duke about Kate and the child, but lied to avoid the marriage:

> *Lucio* I was once before him for getting a wench with child.
> *Duke* Did you such a thing?
> *Lucio* Yes, marry, did I, but I was fain to forswear it. They
>   would else have married me to the rotten medlar.
>   (4.3.168–72)

Lucio, like the husbands of enforced marriages, will not have his desire compelled, and like Stubbes's "scurvie boy" he will show Kate a fair pair of heels. At the end of the play, however, the Duke makes use of the knowledge of Lucio's tricks he gained while in disguise:

> Proclaim it, Provost, round the city,
> If any woman wrong'd by this lewd fellow,
> As I have heard him swear himself there's one
> Whom he begot with child, let her appear,
> And he shall marry her.
>
> (5.1.514–17)

We will discuss the effects of this marriage later. Here we should note that if the Duke began the play as a man more concerned for bastards than for prosecuting sexual crimes, his experience with Lucio and the subculture of Vienna has changed him by the end of the action, when he seeks to control sexuality through forced marriage. During the course of the play the Duke moves from viewing bastardy as a human problem to seeing it as a sexual evil to be controlled by marriage.

In this change of attitude, Vincentio comes to agree with Stubbes and Angelo that the problem is really fornication. These contrasting approaches are revealed in a scene with the Provost and Angelo (2.2). The Provost is sympathetic to Claudio and wonders what will become of the "groaning Juliet," who is very near her time. The Provost's motives may at first seem ambiguous. His concern for her seems genuine, yet, like many of the local officers already discussed, he may not wish her to deliver in his prison. Angelo is testy but accedes to the Provost's request that she be cared for, insisting, however, that Juliet's deed be clearly labeled: "See you the fornicatress be remov'd. / Let her have needful, but not lavish means: / There shall be order for't" (25–27). In the next scene the Provost tells Juliet she will be provided for, his compassion having been established. The Duke later pays tribute to the Provost's attitude (4.2.86–87). The scenes define the difference in approach: one caring for life, the other assigning blame for fornication.

Juliet's plight actually results from conditions over
which she has had little control, ones remarkably similar to
those described by historians of marriage in Shakespeare's
time: the intended marriage interrupted by economic circumstances, which sometimes contributed to the bastardy
rate. Claudio says,

> Thus stands it with me: upon a true contract
> I got possession of Julietta's bed.
> You know the lady; she is fast my wife,
> Save that we do the denunciation lack
> Of outward order. This we came not to,
> Only for propagation of a dow'r
> Remaining in the coffer of her friends,
> From whom we thought it meet to hide our love
> Till time had made them for us. But it chances
> The stealth of our most mutual entertainment
> With character too gross is writ on Juliet.
> (1.2.145–55)

Because *Measure* concentrates on the translation of social
problems into sexual issues, no mention is made of Juliet's
child, beyond its confirming evidence of "mutual entertainment." We should not overlook the play's continued emphasis on the mutuality of the relationship of Juliet and Claudio,
which she repeats to the Friar (2.3.26–27). By insisting on
the difference between the Lucio-Kate relationship and that
of Claudio and Juliet, the play emphasizes the fact that
Claudio must suffer for what Lucio has escaped. The human
and social terms are a total contrast, yet legally the relationships are equated. The gentle Claudio pays for Lucio's
defiant profligacy, which evokes but escapes the law.

In another parallel, Mariana's status is also the result of
an abridged contract, where again the loss of her dowry is
reduced by Angelo to terms of sexual corruption:

> *Duke* She should this Angelo have married, was affianced to
> her by oath, and the nuptial appointed; between which
> time of the contract and limit of the solemnity, her

> brother Frederick was wrack'd at sea, having in that
> perish'd vessel the dowry of his sister. But mark how
> heavily this befell to the poor gentlewoman. There she
> lost a noble and renown'd brother, in his love toward
> her ever most kind and natural; with him, the portion
> and sinew of her fortune, her marriage-dowry; with
> both, her combinate husband, this well-seeming Angelo.
> *Isabella* Can this be so? Did Angelo so leave her?
> *Duke* Left her in her tears, and dried not one of them with
> his comfort; swallow'd his vows whole, pretending in
> her discoveries of dishonour.
>
> (3.1.211–25)

The cause of the rupture was economic, but Angelo impugns
Mariana's honor to explain his breach of contract. Although
Angelo probably sought sexual grounds because they were
considered the most compelling reasons to break a marriage
contract,[71] his attitude fits the general one in *Measure*.
Throughout the play there is a tendency to hold sexuality
guilty of all social ills attached to it and thereby justify control
of it by the state. The exercise of power in relation to sexuality turns it into something joyless and destructive. As
Claudio exclaims to Lucio when he is arrested, "Our natures
do pursue, / Like rats that ravin down their proper bane, / A
thirsty evil, and when we drink we die" (1.2.129–31). When
Lucio might be forced to marry the mother of his child, she
becomes "the rotten medlar." As in the plays of enforced
marriage, male desire constrained by society becomes negative from both the constraint and the guilt attached to the
lack of responsibility. This in turn leads to a pejorative view
of women and of desire.

The relationship of Angelo and Isabella is the center of
the degraded notion of desire and the demeaning attitude
toward women. In his attempt to use the power of the state to
force himself upon Isabella, Angelo represents the extreme
form of male rejection of social constraint and responsibility—sex turned into violence. He will, moreover, like Tar-
quin, use Isabella's lack of social power to deny a relationship
to her after he has used her:

> Who will believe thee, Isabel?
> My unsoil'd name, th'austereness of my life,
> My vouch against you, and my place i' th' state
> Will so your accusation overweigh
> That you shall stifle in your own report
> And smell of calumny.
>
> (2.4.154–59)

Isabella's aggressive chastity is the corresponding extreme form of restraint on sexual desire, negatively perceived. Isabella, in fact, accepts Angelo's debased view of women and desire, but she would exempt herself, a novice, from the category and the emotion. Forcing her into his definition of woman is part of what attracts Angelo to her as we learn in this exchange:

> *Angelo* Nay, women are frail too.
> *Isabella* Ay, as the glasses where they view themselves,
>   Which are as easy broke as they make forms.
>   Women? Help Heaven! Men their creation mar
>   In profiting by them. Nay, call us ten times frail,
>   For we are soft as our complexions are,
>   And credulous to false prints.
> *Angelo*   I think it well.
>   And from this testimony of your own sex—
>   Since I suppose we are made no stronger
>   Than faults may shake our frames—let me be bold.
>   I do arrest your words. Be that you are,
>   That is, a woman; if you be more, you're none.
>
> (2.4.124–35)

Isabella's fierce virginity, which protects her from this assault on her identity, also becomes a mirror of its destructive impulse in her rejection of Claudio's pleas and her condemnation of his lust. Although the play carefully distinguishes among the sexual relationships it presents, Isabella truly believes Claudio did the thing he will die for. She accepts Angelo's definitions of the law and of desire. Shakespeare makes her similarity to Angelo clear by echoing his formulation as she later seeks justice for the execution of Claudio. Angelo, she tells the Duke, is an arch-villain: "believe it, royal prince: / If he be less, he's nothing; but he's more / Had I more name for badness" (5.1.56–58). In their reaction to the intensity of negative desire, Angelo and Isabella become dehumanized and render others worse than they can be. That is why they are natural opponents and why Isabella's forgiveness is critical to Angelo's reclamation, and to her own, at the end. Because as a woman she has only negative power, that is, the withholding of love or herself from the sexual exchange, the play allows Isabella to achieve a change of attitude while it must compel Angelo's behavior, but both characters remain finally ambiguous because they are silent and interpreted by the increasingly problematic Duke. More of that later.

The Law

Desire is not the only cause of the problems in *Measure:* laws have not been enforced during the Duke's rule. In this, as in the ways we have already explored, *Measure* is part of a debate about laxity and law enforcement in English life at the time. As we see from Hext's letter to Burghley, quoted above, some observers believed that the large immoral subculture was quite immune to the control of magistrates, that local officers were, in fact, afraid of that growing segment of society. Puritans, like Stubbes, were certain that the church courts, the Bawdy Courts, which had jurisdiction over sexual offenses, were weak and ineffective. Because such courts could exact only penance as punishment, they established norms of behavior, but they were inadequate for purposes of reform:

> If men sometimes attempted to dodge marriage, or support of bastards, the majority of the community saw no reason why they should not be disciplined. (Probably fundamental to contemporary ideas about social discipline was the fear of unregulated sexuality and reproduction in a society which lacked both effective techniques of contraception and the expecta-

tions of sustained economic growth.) The evidence before the courts points to a good deal of "misbehaviour", but it also includes much criticism, implied or explicit, of such behaviour. . . . The church courts, acting against irresponsible and anti-social behaviour, were supported by the general discipline and responsibility of the masses.[72]

The church courts might define sin, but reformers thought them unable to deal with social ills. The secular courts could mete out real punishments, but there seems to have been general agreement with the statement of Hext that law enforcement by civic magistrates was lax. John Howes said one reason for the existence of the wandering poor was "the carelesse and necligent governement as well of the principall governours as other Inferior officers, to whome these things doe chiefely appertaine."[73] In a tract entitled "Provision for the Poore" (1597) Henry Arth wrote about ten causes for the increase in the poor which he had observed: "The tenth sort of poore makers, is the want of execution of those Lawes and orders made for theyr provision, which fault resteth in Magistrates and officers appoynted to that ende, and in many ministers, who ought publikely and privatly to reproove abuses, and put all persons in minde of their duties, yet either they cannot, or will not performe the same, whereby the most do live in disorder: and will not this dealing increase the poore?"[74] Hext was the most eloquent and specific about the limitations of the justices of the peace:

But the greatest fault ys in the inferior mynyster of Iustice, who shold use more ernest indevor to brynge them to the seate of iudgment and iustice, wherein yf every Iustice of peace in England dyd in every of ther devisions quarterly meete and before ther metyng cause a diligent serche to be made for the apprehendinge of all roages and vagrant suspicious persons, And to brynge them before them, where they shold receave the Iudgment of the lawe, and the sturdyest of them that are the most daungerous Comytted to the howse of Correccion or gayle, and at this meetynge inquyre of the defaults of Alehowses which harbor them, of Constables and Tythingmen that suffer them to wander, and of inhabitants that releve them contrary to the lawe, and inflyct punyshment accordinge to the statute, a roage cold hardlye escape.[75]

In short, Hext believed, the laws are adequate if the officers would enforce them. Parliamentary debates contain eloquent testimony about the inferior origins, the poverty, and the partiality of the justices of the peace. The performance of incumbents simply did not inspire confidence, and Parliament was reluctant to give such officers more power through reform legislation.

Furthermore, the character of the king himself, so newly come to the throne, was arousing concern among Englishmen about negligence of government. When it came to hard work and devotion to her country, Elizabeth was a hard act to follow, and it was soon apparent that James preferred hunting to governing, the country to London. In addition, Elizabeth's parsimony had been so extreme that James's bounty made his new subjects nervous. Sir Roger Wilbraham compares the two in 1603: "The King most bountiful, seldome denying any sute: the Quene strict in geving, which age & her sex inclyned her unto: the one often complayned of for sparinge: th'other so benigne, that his people feare his over redines in gevinge."[76] James lacked the will and the skill to convince the English that he cared about them, whatever his theories about the king as father to his subjects:

> He loves quiet and repose, has little inclination to war, nay is opposed to it, a fact that little pleases many of his subjects, though it pleases them still less that he leaves all government to his Council and will think of nothing but the chase. He does not caress the people or make them that good cheer the late Queen did, whereby she won their loves: for the English adore their Sovereigns, and if the King passed through the same street a hundred times a day the people would still run to see him; they like their King to show pleasure at their devotion, as the late Queen knew well how to do; but this King manifests no taste for them but rather contempt and dislike.[77]

Although James was jealous of his perogatives, he was seldom harsh in assessing penalties. In fact, his clemency quickly became legendary. He accompanied the first execution of his reign, that of a cutpurse in New-warke upon Trent, with a pardon of "all the other poore and wretched Prisoners, clearing the Castle of them all."[78] Later in 1603 James's eleventh-hour pardons of Sir Griffin Markham, Lord Grey, and Lord Cobham read like the ending of a tragicomedy. The prisoners were escorted to the scaffold, the sheriff made a short speech about the heinousness of their crimes, to which they consented, "then saith the Sheriff, 'See the mercy of your Prince, who of himself hath sent hither to countermand, and given you your lives!' "[79]

Then, too, James's court quickly became notorious for its sexual corruption. As early as 1603 Lady Anne Clifford remarked, "Now there was much talk of a masque the Queen had at Winchester and how all the ladies about the court had gotten such ill names that it was grown a scandalous place, and the Queen herself was much fallen from her former greatness and reputation she had in the world."[80] Other public criticism was tolerated by the king and enjoyed by the queen, as the French ambassador reported caricatures of the king in plays and sermons against him as early as June 1604.[81]

This sense of laxity from top to bottom produced a general wish to control personal behavior, particularly sexual offenses. The impulse took several forms. As we have seen, there were harsher punishments for bastardy under existing laws; localities adopted laws making marriage and settlement in towns more difficult; and local authorities gradually became more conscientious, especially with regard to the sexual offenses of the subculture that produced many social problems:

> Village officers, who in the period before 1607 had been themselves deeply involved in the popular culture which produced bastardy and who had turned a blind eye to minor misdemeanours, were replaced by men of a different stamp. . . .

Concern with the disorders of the poor also involved the closer regulation of sexual and marital behaviour. Sexual incontinency unrelated to an actual pregnancy and therefore to a potentially chargeable bastard child, was infrequently prosecuted in the church courts before 1607. Thereafter prosecutions of sexual irregularities of this kind were a more regular feature of Terling presentments. In particular prenuptial fornication which had become evident only *after* marriage, was never presented before 1609. In subsequent years it was quite frequently presented, especially in the later 1620s.[82]

Meanwhile, from 1576 to 1628, Parliament was debating ninety-five proposed laws which would control personal conduct: regulations of dress, drinking, swearing, bastardy, church attendance, and honoring the Sabbath.[83] Most of these bills were sponsored by Puritan members of Commons, and the debate reveals awareness of many of the issues explored in *Measure*. Bills passed if they addressed social problems rather than the morals of subjects: "Despite the eagerness of Puritan members like Robert Wroth and William Wiseman to punish the begetting of a bastard as a sin, regardless of its social implications, the provisions enacted by the Commons continued to distinguish between parents who agreed to provide for the child and those who left it to be maintained by the parish."[84] Therefore, Parliamentary debates made a distinction which Shakespeare represents as crucial to the problem: does the male, like Claudio, assume responsibility for his action, or does he, like Lucio or Angelo, deny it? That is a fundamental distinction for Parliament and for *Measure*. For the majority of Parliament the distinction is important because, unlike Stubbes or Angelo, they wished to separate social problems from morality: although both Juliet and Kate Keepdown must be provided for, their pregnancies cannot be equated. Not that members really worried greatly about women; their concern really lay with the consequences for men of the increased severity of penalties: the impact on the social order and the partiality of officers, for whom members had little respect:

> Some members feared that one or two justices . . . would act
> out of malice or ill will, passion or self-interest, and that they
> would show little regard for social distinctions in the exercise
> of their authority. Henry Unton's concern in 1593 that gen-
> tlemen would be punished under the bastardy laws stemmed
> in part from the fact that their enforcement was left to two
> justices who, he claimed, might be prompted by malice to
> convict those accused by whores. George More's fear that
> gentlemen who were disordered or drunk might be sent to a
> house of correction to be whipped was occasioned by his dis-
> trust of the summary jurisdiction of one justice.[85]

This concern for the social order is basic to the debates about
the proposed laws; members feared the power such measures would give socially inferior justices over gentlemen.
Members assumed that the social problems were created almost entirely by the sexual offenses of the poor, and that
these, not the peccadillos of gentle folk, should be the focus
of the legislation. In fact, bills were specifically designed to be
class conscious:

> Some of the bills attributed the offences which they were
> designed to punish particularly to the meaner sort of people
> and were probably meant largely for the discipline of the
> poor. Other bills seem to have been intended for the regula-
> tion of the conduct of all classes in society; in at least one case
> the penalties were graded according to the social degree of
> the offender, while several bills allowed a range of penalties
> though it was not stipulated that they be imposed in accor-
> dance with social position. A number of members regarded
> such provisions as a threat to the maintenance of social dis-
> tinctions. In particular, they feared that regulations would be
> applied to "gentlemen" or "the better sort", and they consid-
> ered it inappropriate to punish these classes for such of-
> fenses.[86]

Members were also sensitive to the partiality and frailty
of magistrates. One speaker might have been describing Angelo: "For magistrates are men, and men have always at-
tending on them two ministers, *libido* and *iracunda*. Men in

this nature do subjugate the free subject."[87] Members and other commentators feared that a reaction to previous laxity might result in the hunting of sin and the meting of partial justice, particularly among the Puritan segment of the society. It was this spirit of detecting "enormities" combined with Puritan zeal that Ben Jonson satirized ten years later in *Bartholomew Fayre* (1614), his parody on the disguised-ruler play. John Howes also gives an eloquent statement of the danger that sin-hunting could distract society from the care of the needy:

> I lyke well to have synne punnyshed, but not parceallye. They see in the streates a nomber of poore, aged and lame in greate myserye, but that they can not remedie. They see in the streates a nomber of poore children lye under stalles all the yere longe. They see dyvers poore woemen delyvered of childe in the streates, churches and cadges, and no provision for them. They have sene allso a great nomber of poore men, which have died this sommer of the sycknes in the streate for wante of reliefe, and no place provided for them. These things are to to apparent in the eies of the people, that heaven and earthe cryeth vengeance, and suerly god can not be angrie with us that will suffer our Christian Bretheran to die in the streates for want of relyefe, and wee spend and consume our wealthe and our wytte in searching out Harlotts, and leave the worckes of faythe and mercie undone.[88]

Because Howes's concern for the poor is deeply felt and because Parliament made genuine social considerations the primary goal of regulating personal conduct, within its social lights, to be sure, we should give credit to Elizabethan and Jacobean Englishmen who passed the Poor Laws and other legislation to provide for the old, sick, and unemployed. With all their flaws and callous enforcement, they were a unique achievement for a western nation: "This system of national tax-supported poor relief, which got under way on a systematic scale in about 1600 and grew steadily in scope and cost thereafter, was one of the more important single differences between England and the Continent."[89]

Stern Measures

Measure addresses many of the issues in this debate about the relation of law to personal conduct. Features of the play frequently represent the fears of Shakespeare's contemporaries, and by concentrating the issue on sexuality, a natural strategy in comedy, Shakespeare explores the limits of the problem. Vienna has been governed leniently, and its local officers are clearly inadequate to their responsibilities. His previous laxity is the Duke's acknowledged reason for assuming a disguise and giving Angelo a chance to institute greater severity without being accused of tyranny because of having "caused" the offenses against the law through leniency. When the Duke speaks to Friar Thomas of the twigs of birch becoming "more mock'd than fear'd" (1.3.24–27), we recall Hext's scoundrels laughing up their sleeves at local officers. As he struggles to make sense of Elbow's fractured language, Escalus becomes aware of how Elbow is manipulated by the likes of Pompey and of the strong need for better officers:

> *Escalus* Come hither to me, Master Elbow; come hither,
>   Master Constable. How long have you been in this place
>   of constable?
> *Elbow* Seven year and a half, sir.
> *Escalus* I thought, by your readiness in the office, you had
>   continued in it some time. You say, seven years
>   together?
> *Elbow* And a half, sir.
> *Escalus* Alas, it hath been great pains to you. They do you
>   wrong to put you so oft upon't. Are there not men in
>   your ward sufficient to serve it?
> *Elbow* Faith, sir, few of any wit in such matters. As they are
>   chosen, they are glad to choose me for them. I do it for
>   some piece of money, and go through with all.
> *Escalus* Look you bring me in the names of some six or
>   seven, the most sufficient of your parish.
> *Elbow* To your worship's house, sir?
> *Escalus* To my house. Fare you well.
>
>   (2.1.255–72)

In this context, Angelo's severity can seem a welcome response to any audience, but Shakespeare soon weights it with all the dangers feared by his contemporaries: partiality, sin-hunting, and disruption of the social order. Instead of concentrating on the irresponsible Lucios of Vienna, Angelo, driven by *libido* and *iracundia,* pursues Claudio, who mirrors Angelo's own flaws. Shakespeare stresses the disruption of the social order which Angelo's decision causes by emphasizing Claudio's gentle station: Escalus first pleads with Angelo about Claudio: "Alas, this gentleman / Whom I would save, had a most noble father!" (2.1.6–7). And before he thinks Claudio must die, Escalus tells the Duke-friar, "I have labor'd for the poor gentleman to the extremest shore of my modesty, but my brother justice have I found so severe, that he hath forc'd me to tell him he is indeed Justice" (3.2.244–48). Up until the last moment the Provost says of a knock at the door, "I hope it is some pardon or reprieve / For the most gentle Claudio" (4.2.71–72). The action Shakespeare contrives epitomizes parliamentary fears that laws meant to restrain Pompey or Lucio would fall instead on Claudio, often because of the partiality of the magistrates. The play gradually reveals how close Claudio's situation is to Angelo's. Both are parties to marriage contracts interrupted by problems with dowries, and Claudio has acted out Angelo's guilty desires, which the deputy must punish. Yet Angelo's attempted victimization of Claudio and Isabella is not the extreme representation of social disorder or the intrusion of the state into personal life. The limits of both ideas lie in the theme of no difference and the bed trick.[90]

Shakespeare builds the theme of no difference into a terrifying idea as he associates the law, sex, and death as elements of life which obliterate identity, the distinctions among persons. The Duke-friar's substitutions link the law, death, and sex in this suggestion of no difference: he uses substitutions to replace Angelo's law with a more merciful version, to replace Claudio as Angelo's intended victim of execution with one who has died naturally, and to replace an intended rape victim with a contracted wife. The law, Angelo hypocritically tells Isabella, falls on all individuals equally: "Be you content, fair maid. / It is the law, not I, condemn your brother. / Were he my kinsman, brother, or my son, / It should be thus with him" (2.2.83–86). Angelo's character should not distract us from the truth that the law does efface individuality; as it deals with classes and actions, justice needs seasoning with the mercy of the individual circumstances.

When the Provost and the Duke-friar need a head to substitute for Claudio's, they convince themselves that Angelo will not know Barnardine's head from Claudio's: "O, death's a great disguiser, and you may add to it," the Duke-friar tells the Provost. Earlier in the same scene Abhorson explains the mystery of the hangman to Pompey in terms of no difference: "Every true man's apparel fits your thief. If it be too little for your thief, your true man thinks it big enough; if it be too big for your thief, your thief thinks it little enough. So every true man's apparel fits your thief" (4.2.43–47). The word play and choplogic efface the distinctions in the language itself, as the varied meanings of "too little" and "little enough" become intentionally blurred.

The theme of no difference is most powerfully evoked, however, in the Duke-friar's bed trick which lies at the center of *Measure*. For the bed trick to work, one woman must be like another to the lustful male in the dark. As we have already noted, the bed trick is the most disturbing element in *Measure* because the state intrudes directly in sexual intercourse, which is "rendered transparent to the eyes of the sovereign and audience."[91] The bed trick is the true mirror of Angelo's attempt to use the power of the state to rape Isabella. Although Shakespeare tries to mitigate its effect, we should trust the discomfort centuries of playgoers have experienced with the device. By discussing it in great detail, Shakespeare calls our attention to its problems.

First, there is the fact that neither Isabella nor Vincentio is party to the act, as is Helena in *All's Well*. Shakespeare devotes almost half a scene to Vincentio's explanation to Isabella about Mariana's plight and the justice of her cause (3.1.184–280). Isabella does not instantly agree to the device, but only after careful argument from a holy man. Second, we are assured that Mariana still loves Angelo, despite the fact that he has behaved very badly toward her and accused her of unchastity. Third, and most important, Mariana has "title" to Angelo by precontract. For five years, she has been like Clare in *The Miseries of Enforced Marriage*, betrothed to a man who did not marry her, her life ended, no other relationship possible, immured in the moated grange. For Mariana, then, the bed trick is liberation from an impossible status, and if it serves other good purposes too, she agrees to her chance for life. Shakespeare is here still dealing with a version of the patient wife in Mariana, who will redeem her prodigal husband by forgiveness, thus saving his life. Yet the ability of the Duke to take liberties with individual autonomy while he is disguised as the friar, liberties he could not take with all his public power as ruler, remains problematic and frightening. Shakespeare's fellow dramatists who made the disguised ruler spy on his own children saw far less deeply into the implications of patriarchal power than did Shakespeare. If the ruler's authority derived from the father-child relationship, some control of the children's sexual lives was implied, but here Shakespeare tested the limits of the theory and made them disturbing. The autonomy of the individual is lost to the design of the sovereign, and male desire is used to compel its own conformity. In thinking he is committing fornication, Angelo has consummated a marriage he had rejected.

Marriage

In *Measure* only Claudio and Juliet make their own marriage; the Duke makes all the others at the end of the action. *Measure* suffers from the radical divorce of marriage from desire, and the intrusion of power into the relationship makes marriage problematic. As the single institution to regulate the complexities of sexual desire, marriage is subject to almost intolerable strains at the end of *Measure:* how can a single institution deal with the vagaries of male sexuality rep-

resented in Angelo, Claudio, Lucio, and even Vincentio himself? Once marriage ceases to be the fulfillment of desire,
especially for the male, and becomes a regulatory agency in
society, usually on behalf of women, it intrudes power into
sexuality. Marriage no longer means love for an individual
or, more broadly, one's heart's desire; instead it becomes a
matter of contracts, rights, and titles, which seem to protect
women—insofar as that is possible, and certainly to constrain
men—insofar as that is possible. The ruler uses the patriarchal power of making marriages on behalf of women to
coerce men into social responsibility, against which most rebel. *All's Well* presents a structure which attempts to resolve
the conflict between marriage as a personal relationship and
as an instrument of patriarchal power. Instead of resolving
these conflicts *Measure* accents the tensions between power
and sexuality in marriage.

The fact that Angelo has been tricked into consummat-
ing his marriage does not make his contract any less real to
Mariana, who has already been assured about her "title" by
the Duke-friar, who rationalizes the deceit of the bed trick
through the contract. She says,

> This is that face, thou cruel Angelo,
> Which once thou swor'st was worth the looking on;
> This is the hand which, with a vow'd contract,
> Was fast belock'd in thine; this is the body
> That took away the match from Isabel,
> And did supply thee at thy garden-house
> In her imagin'd person.
>   (5.1.211–17)

Angelo's insistence that he has not seen or spoken to Mariana
in five years matters little to her: "I am affianc'd this man's
wife as strongly / As words could make up vows" (5.1.231–
32). Angelo insists rightly and condescendingly that Isabella
and Mariana are "but instruments of some more mightier
member / That sets them on" (242–43). The willingness of
Angelo to misuse the power of the state to indulge his own

desire finds an answering fixity of purpose in the Duke, who, after Angelo confesses his guilt, orders him to marry Mariana formally at once. Thus, the power of the state supports female desire and constrains that of the male, and marriage is closely associated with punishment for the male. Yet, having confessed his guilt, Angelo needs Mariana as the patient wife to save his life and to earn the forgiveness of both Isabella and the Duke. The relationships are made so complex by the past and there is so little time for reconciliation that marriage seems like a benign prison, not unlike the immured garden or the moated grange in which the Duke places his subjects to keep them out of trouble.

For the irresponsible Lucio marriage is a sentence, a punishment which he has escaped once before. This marriage is entirely one of the Duke's will to provide for Lucio's bastard, for the invisible, voiceless Kate Keepdown is never present to ask for marriage, nor is her protector, Mistress Overdone. This is the clearest example of the use of marriage as a social agency by the ruler: "Marrying a punk, my lord, is pressing to death, whipping, and hanging" (278–79). The invisibility of Kate Keepdown reveals the extent to which in this context marriage, like cuckoldry, is an affair between men using women as counters. Here Vincentio needs to control Lucio's flouting of authority, largely his slander of Vincentio himself, and forces the marriage upon him as a punishment, a legalized revenge. Thus are women and desire a means of the enforcement of the subject's will to the ruler's design.

Are not these unions made at the express command of the Duke forced marriages? Clearly, but now without the structure in *All's Well* which can gradually ameliorate the relationships. By reverting to the pattern of romantic comedy with the multiple marriages at the end, but with the marriages divorced from desire, Shakespeare makes even more striking the basic instability and tenuousness of the relationships, which exist by the ruler's order and trickery. Matheo's rebellion in *The Honest Whore, Part II* is an indication that forced marriages cannot not be depended upon, simply because they end comedies, and in *Measure* only Claudio and Juliet have a marriage of desire. Vincentio's injunctions to Angelo to love Mariana convey an anxiety about their relationship: "Look that you love your wife; her worth worth yours. . . . Love her, Angelo. / I have confess'd her and I know her virtue" (5.1.502, 530). The Duke's fussiness about love is just enough to remind us that it is absent on Angelo's part and on Lucio's part too. Angelo, moreover, is quite silent after his last plea for execution.

Although marriage may be a contract in which women have rights which the ruler will support, when the relationship is enforced, we expect the husband to rebel against it and the enforcing authority. This is another reason why marriage is a poor institution to regulate sexuality: it really cannot control male desire. Only when the male is finally reconciled to it does the forced marriage survive. Therefore, like *The Malcontent* or *The Phoenix*, *Measure* ends with the strong suggestion that constraint of sexuality by patriarchal authority is largely illusory, that sexuality is the "worst case" for testing the limits of state authority in regulating personal conduct.

One final proposal of marriage raises another set of questions: Vincentio's offer of himself to the entirely silent Isabella. Because the proposal comes after the revelation that Vincentio has saved Claudio's life, the Duke's substitution of himself for Angelo cannot be lost on the audience. The gesture seems particularly callous, for although Isabella learns humility in the course of the action, the play does not imply that her chastity is less dear to her at the end. I wish to argue that Isabella's silence may be a compound of shock and defiance. She has known nothing of the Duke's feelings for her, and we have other examples in Iago and Hieronimo, where silence after eloquence may signify not acquiescence, but defiance of an urgent authority. Because he controls all else, the Duke expects Isabella to abandon, casually because he wishes it, the celibate identity she has been unwilling to sacrifice for her brother's life. It should not escape us that in proposing to her, the Duke reverts to the friar's mode of behavior and substitutes himself for Angelo, who would have forced himself upon Isabella.[92] Although he offers marriage instead of fornication, the gesture should be read as a tyrannical one to which Isabella's reaction is still an open question as the play ends.

The Patriarchal Ruler

Duke Vincentio has remained a puzzle for interpreters of *Measure*. Richard Wheeler's description is representative: "Shakespeare strands Vincentio in a kind of allegorical no-man's-land, a shadowy figure of justice tempered with mercy, but a lover without plausible desire, a father with no children, a renouncer with nothing in him to renounce, an empty center precariously holding at a distance, rather than holding together, the teeming life that threatens to overwhelm it."[93] My argument is that Shakespeare's representation of the contradictions of patriarchal power in Vincentio accounts for the paradoxical effect of the play in general: it seems sui generis and yet a member of a well-defined subgenre; it was performed for James I and yet contains a deeply ambiguous figure as a ruler. By splitting the ruler into duke and friar Shakespeare at once gives the ruler enormous power and exposes the tyrannical nature of that power. Although Vincentio is not the literal father of those whom he observes, Shakespeare continues the patriarchal metaphor by having Vincentio become a holy father who ministers and confesses those on whom he spies. The disguise allows Vincentio to intrude his power into the dark corners of his realm so that he is at once a trickster in his magical substitutions[94] and a god, who uses the knowledge he has gained as a friar to trap Lucio and Angelo when once again the Duke. Thus he has seemed to critics, as to Angelo, a providential figure: "I perceive your Grace, like pow'r divine, / Hath look'd upon my passes" (5.1.374–75). This is the ultimate fantasy of the father-ruler: his subjects' lives are transparent and under magical control. Yet we must resist making Angelo's (or James's) Vincentio our own. The disguise exposes the limits of public power and the fantasy of intruding power into the personal realm.[95] Vincentio is frightening because at the end he blends the private, religious power of the friar and the public power of the Duke without the constraints of either one. As Duke he lacks knowledge of Lucio's passes, and, however godlike, he rules visibly and within law. As friar he is ruled by his holy vows; he acts in accordance with divine authority, subduing earthly passions. His actions, like divine power, may be invisible. The composite figure of the Duke-friar approaches James's definition of the king in *The Basilicon Doron:* "God gives not Kings the stile of *Gods* in vaine, / For on his throne his Scepter do they sway: / And as their subjects ought them to obey, / So Kings should feare and serve their God again."[96] By splitting the figure Shakespeare shows how this concept of the ruler mixes secular and religious power and tends to deny the constraints of both. It confuses being a man of god with being like a god, and it justifies control of the subject's intimate life according to the ruler's design. It also illustrates how important a limit on power is its sheer visibility, its being public and not secret.[97] When he is justifying the bed trick Vincentio presents the issue in terms of the ruler's morality and hypocrisy:

> He who the sword of heaven will bear
> Should be as holy as severe;
> Pattern in himself to know,
> Grace to stand, and virtue go;
> More nor less to others paying
> Than by self-offences weighing.
> Shame to him whose cruel striking
> Kills for faults of his own liking!
> . . . .
> O, what may man within him hide,
> Though angel on the outward side!
> How may likeness made in crimes,
> Making practice on the times,
> To draw with idle spiders' strings

Most ponderous and substantial things!
Craft against vice I must apply.
                                                        (3.2.254–70)

The rhetoric of divine authority can use hypocrisy (who but
God knows our true hearts?) to justify secret delving into
private lives by a holy man, whose sanction is ministering to
souls. But this friar will use craft to enforce a contract—he
will substitute Mariana for Isabella to "pay with falsehood
false exacting / And perform an old contracting" (3.2.274–
75). Vincentio's formulation applies as much to himself as to
Angelo: he uses Angelo's crimes to justify his deceit; his substitutions accept the letter of the law (old contracting) to
victimize others; as he would force Isabella at the end, he
punishes Angelo for his own fault. Although the result of the
Duke-friar's manipulations seems benign, the play is full of
suggestions that he becomes tyrannical. By the end of the
play the Duke seeks to punish in Angelo a mirror of his own
tyranny, just as Angelo has sought to punish Claudio, who
mirrors his desires. The process by which Vincentio evolves
into a tyrant deserves review.

We have two sources of information about what the Duke
was like before his disguise: the unreliable Lucio and the
reliable Escalus. For Lucio the Duke was indulgent, nurturing, merciful—he would never have executed Claudio. Although Lucio imputes Vincentio's mercy to a taste for sport
that seems entirely Lucio's fiction, we find little reason to
doubt the Duke's caring nature. Escalus speaks of a self-
conscious, temperate man: "One that, above all other strifes,
contended especially to know himself. . . . Rather rejoicing to
see another merry, than merry at any thing which profess'd to
make him rejoice; a gentleman of all temperance" (3.2.227–
32). Yet after fourteen years this caring, temperate man wants
stricter law enforcement, but he fears that it would be tyrannical of him to do so and so he displaces that responsibility on
Angelo, "who may, in th'ambush of my name, strike home, /
And yet my nature never in the fight / To do in slander"
(1.3.41–43). Although Vincentio's plan is that he will preserve

his reputation while Angelo will bear all the resentment for stricter enforcement, Vincentio is greatly changed by his experience ministering to the denizens of prison. After he has been in the prison for a short time, we find the Duke-friar exclaiming, "O heavens, what stuff is here?" (3.2.5), and he condemns Pompey, the cheerful bawd, in the sternest tones:

> Fie, sirrah, a bawd, a wicked bawd!
> The evil that thou causest to be done,
> That is thy means to live. Do thou but think
> What 'tis to cram a maw or clothe a back
> From such a filthy vice; say to thyself,
> From their abominable and beastly touches
> I drink, I eat, array myself, and live.
> Canst thou believe thy living is a life,
> So stinkingly depending?
>
> (20–28)

After Pompey has made the telling distinction between prostitution, which is illegal, and usury, which is legal, Vincentio's sentiments seem simplistic and harsh. Ironically, even though Vincentio can see Angelo's severities, his own escape him. He seems to care about what happens to women: he tries to save Isabella's chastity and Mariana's destiny, but the bed trick compels Angelo's desire. He remembers Kate Keepdown, but forces Lucio to a relationship that is like whipping and hanging. Vincentio is changed by his encounters with the hardcore offenders of his realm, and this experience makes him as strict as the deputy he calls tyrant.

In his effort to reform his city, Vincentio uses the modes of both roles he occupies. The problem is that the friar can deal with sin and love, but the ruler can deal only with the law and marriage. Vincentio does not respect these limits, and his shifts from one to the other are disquieting.[98] For example, his willingness to use confession as evidence is disturbing. He tells Claudio that he knows Angelo was testing Isabella: "I am confessor to Angelo, and I know this to be true" (3.1.165–66). Later he says casually that he knows of

Mariana's virtue because he has confessed her (5.1.531). This abuse of a religious role would be trivial, especially in a disguised character, except for the bed trick and Vincentio's entrapment of Lucio about lying to the Duke in court. We might rejoice at the success of the friar's trickster, backstairs work in outwitting an oppressive authority, if he were not himself the authority with a design of his own.

It becomes very hard to separate the caring from the punitive in Vincentio's conduct. His substitutions result in mercy, but they also follow the letter of the law, quite the opposite of the concept of waiving the law for humane reasons. The blending of the roles is even more serious with regard to passion. Throughout the play the Duke has been established as reserved and temperate in his emotions, an excellent thing in a ruler.[99] The friar should be celibate: he should be above the passions of ordinary mortals. By his own principles, Vincentio should be passionless if he is not to punish his own sins. Yet, like Angelo, the Duke is attracted to Isabella, and in yielding to that desire, Vincentio reveals his fundamental similarity to Angelo, even without the further gesture, discussed earlier, of substituting himself for the deputy in proposing to Isabella. Although his language is not erotic in the least, Vincentio's persistence in repeating the proposal in light of Isabella's silence makes the change difficult to ignore. To summarize, Vincentio becomes tyrannical as he abuses the friar's role to extend his power beyond the law and as he becomes like Angelo in yielding to his attraction to Isabella. The pardons he offers to Angelo, Lucio, and Isabella should not alter this conclusion. In their staginess they bear an uncanny resemblance to James's last-minute clemencies, and they are transparently part of Vincentio's design.

We may now better understand why James could find *Measure* appealing, and audiences find it disturbing. Not only does it have many surface features that are consonant with James's known views, such as Vincentio's distaste for crowds, but also the play accords the ruler enormous power without overt criticism.[100] All reservations about Vincentio's conduct are subversive elements or contradictions within the text, and as such they need not have bothered a royal audience, which was generally tolerant of criticism even if it was quite blatant. *Measure* would have interested James because it is about patriarchal power, a subject about which he wrote and thought more than any other. If its approaches to the theme are fundamentally interrogative, they need hardly have troubled the king and they can fascinate posterity. That *Measure* has always seemed unique and yet is closely allied to many similar plays written at the same time should be our first clue to its essentially subversive character: by the crucial change of having Vincentio unrelated to any characters into whose private lives he delves, Shakespeare makes the disguised-ruler structure radically problematic. That is why the play which is so similar to the others seems really different—it is. Yet, one knows the difference largely by reading it against the others.

It is with some relief, then, that we contemplate the fact that in *Measure* (as in *The Phoenix, The Malcontent,* or *Bartholomew Fayre*) the patriarchal ruler, no matter how powerful, cannot finally control sexuality, that the teeming life Wheeler sees as almost overwhelming Vincentio is stubbornly resistant to order. Vincentio cannot finally spay and geld all the youth of Vienna, and although a lack of reform implies great suffering, especially for women, it is preferable to the loss of personal autonomy to the sovereign.[101] *Measure* represents a crisis in Shakespeare's views of sexuality, which is never again in his comedies free from questions of the state. In the romances ruler-fathers attempt to control its vagaries for the sake of their succession.

CHAPTER THREE

The Romances: Patriarchy, Pure and Simple

At the end of *James I and the Politics of Literature* Jonathan Goldberg compares *Cymbeline* to the ceilings of Inigo Jones's Banqueting House at Whitehall, painted by Rubens for Charles I to "summarize his father's reign and provide a justification for his own." Goldberg catalogues the numerous resemblances of *Cymbeline* to "the style of the gods," which James and Charles used to convey the dominant ideology of their reigns: an emphasis on peace between Britain and the Rome of Augustus Caesar; the king's sons coming from Wales; Imogen's bearing the name of Brut's wife; Posthumus's dream of Jupiter; a king who describes himself as giving birth to his children and forgiving all as a loving "nourishe-father." Yet before listing these elements Goldberg hastens to add that *Cymbeline* does not have "the same aim as the Whitehall paintings."[1] Although the argument of this chapter will relate Shakespeare's last plays to the political discourse of Jacobean England, it should not be taken to imply

111

that Shakespeare is an apologist for the views of James or that the romances are narrowly topical—that they simply reproduce the history of their times. Instead, my argument will be that the romances represent power in terms to be illuminated by the political discourse of their time, but they are not captive of any single perspective, that of James or any other thinker. The terms they use are common but hardly monolithic. The Stuart ideology uses patriarchal ideas and a complex mystique to support its claims to absolute authority; Shakespeare's romances maintain their autonomy by using a similar language to represent power in a way that both conforms to and critiques the Stuart representation. As usual, Shakespeare presents the range of ideas in his age, but commits himself finally to none of them.

Through reversion to the genre of romance, Shakespeare's last plays mythologize patriarchal power, making its structures seem innocent, making them virtually disappear into a providential cosmos and the most natural of power relationships, the family. Although they do not seem to be so—and that concealment is part of their strategy—*Pericles* (1608), *Cymbeline* (1611), *The Winter's Tale* (1611), and *The Tempest* (1611) are deeply political. Each presents a father-ruler or a series of them. In the course of the action, the families of the rulers are almost destroyed, but their final reunion assures the succession within the domain, usually through the daughter, who marries a suitable mate. The patriarchal ideology which lies at the center of the romances may be described briefly; some of its elements are more easily discerned than others. The basis of the social order is found in nature, frequently a providential nature, beneficent to human values. The father's natural authority within the family is the model for his political power, which may be, as in *The Tempest*, magical control over an island. The absolute power of the ruler to control the lives of others is unquestioned in these plays, for most of the subjects are his family or close retainers. Although the ruler or his doubles may at first be tyrannical, he transcends that impulse. This change of attitude does not lessen his power, however. (Here *The*

Tempest is an exception.) Rather, he chooses not to use it in pardoning those who have wronged him, so that the plays end with a vision of the peaceful succession of the next generation. From this admittedly reductive summary it should be apparent to the reader that Shakespeare's romances do not move beyond *Lear;* instead they recapitulate the themes and questions of the tragedy. These themes are, as I hope to demonstrate in this chapter, part of the larger political discourse of the early Stuart era and, in *The Tempest,* a critique of its ideology.

Like *Lear* each romance also exposes possible threats to the patriarchal order; but, unlike the tragedy, these plays use the genre of romance to allay such anxieties. That is why Prospero must give up his magical power at the end of *The Tempest:* the resolutions of the other plays are part of the illusory world of romance. The most immediate threat to society is the abuse of the ruler's enormous power by the ruler or his counterparts, such as Antiochus in *Pericles.* The plays destroy such tyrants or change them if they are heroes such as Leontes or Cymbeline. The problem of the ruler's weakness is also glanced at in Cymbeline or Cleon where their misdeeds are blamed on their wives. With the ruler's authority based in the family, incest is a terrifying specter, directly raised in *Pericles* and hinted at in *The Winter's Tale* and *Cymbeline.* The destruction of the family, sexual infidelity, and the loss of heirs all hover at the center of these plays. The power of women, derived from their generativity and the importance of the family, may be evil or may seem so to the ruler: it must be controlled in the service of the realm. The patriarchy always seeks to appropriate to itself the reproductive powers of women. And most basic of all, what if nature itself is a source of disorder and social discord? In *The Tempest* this prospect serves to demystify the myth created in the other plays, that providential nature lies at the bottom of the social order.

Roland Barthes's essay "Myth Today" is helpful in understanding how Shakespeare uses the concept of nature in the romances. After having explored the limitations of providential images of nature in *Lear, Coriolanus,* or *Troilus and Cressida,* Shakespeare returns to that earlier vision of nature in *Pericles, Cymbeline,* and *The Winter's Tale.* If we seek an answer to David Bevington's question about the romances, "Why did he turn to such old-fashioned models in 1608–10?"[2] we may find one explanation in Shakespeare's mythologizing patriarchal structures according to the process described by Barthes. Myth, Barthes says, "transforms history into Nature." Through this process, Barthes explains, political institutions that are historically contingent may be represented as universal, eternal, unchangeable. Such a representation mystifies, but it does not explain: "Myth does not deny things, on the contrary, its function is to talk about them; simply, it purifies them, it makes them innocent, it gives them a natural and eternal justification, it gives them a clarity which is not that of an explanation but that of a statement of fact."[3] Myth, Barthes says, is depoliticized speech: thus we see the function of the court masque or the pastoral in rendering political ideologies pure and simple. From Barthes's formulation we can understand why the sea washes up Pericles's armor, why Imogen finds her brothers on the way to Milford Haven, or why the son of Polixenes finds Leontes's daughter among the shepherds of Bohemia. We can also understand why the romances can be political without seeming to be. In *Pericles, Cymbeline,* and *The Winter's Tale* nature is not only at the bottom of history, but myth is directly evoked by the appearance of Diana, of Jupiter, and in the use of the oracle.

By shifting in *The Tempest* to a familiar, but radically different concept of nature, a source of occult power and a violent disorder, Shakespeare reveals the myth-making which was almost transparent in the earlier romances and shows it to be a product, not of providence, but of human wish. Through the contrast between the barren island, home of a witch and her monster son, and Prospero's creation of fecund Nature in the wedding masque (here Ceres and Iris appear under human auspices), Shakespeare demonstrates to his audience how a beneficent or providential nature may be a product of the human imagination. That is at least one implication of making the tempest itself, conventionally a providential agent, the creation of a magus.

Indeed, as he composed the romances, Shakespeare also included elements that alert the audience to the fact that they are witnessing a theatrical spectacle, an awareness that can balance the naturalizing of the political structures. If one views the romances chronologically, one finds an increasing emphasis on the fact that the plays are imaginative creations, which continually insist they are contrived artifacts. Gower presents the old story in *Pericles,* and dramatic technique constantly calls attention to itself in *Cymbeline.* The theme becomes quite emphatic in *The Winter's Tale,* where it is most strongly associated with the appearance of Time, with Paulina's magic, and with echoes of the title scattered through other parts of the play as well. *The Tempest* presents the stage audience with a series of spectacles and then at the end reminds the theater audience of the power of its imagination.

The romances also include elements that alert the audience to the fact that they are witnessing not just a theatrical spectacle, but a special myth-making of the Barthian sort. One means of creating such awareness is moving from myth to history at the end of the play, as in *Cymbeline* when the peace is made with Rome and the audience becomes conscious that Cymbeline was ruling Britain at the moment when Christ was born, that an event with eternal implications took place at a historical moment. Prospero's renunciation of his island magic for the ordinary dukedom of Milan is another such transition.

This effect is also achieved by contradictory elements within the text, scenes in a style not entirely compatible with the mythic structures. The brothel scenes of *Pericles* are an example of discourse quite diverse from the rest of the play. The rejection of the pastoral by Avirargus and Guiderius almost destroys its significance in *Cymbeline.* Similarly the social mobility of Perdita's foster family blatantly contradicts the natural nobility represented in Florizel and Perdita. *The Tempest* invites the audience to assume that Prospero's island will represent a utopia, only to mock Gonzalo's description of such an ideal society. All these effects will be analyzed in greater detail throughout this chapter.

As we have already suggested, Shakespeare invented neither the patriarchal ideology represented in the romances nor the practice of mythologizing it through nature. Although the relation of these plays to the political discourse of early Stuart England has been neglected, it is useful to understand why Shakespeare might have turned to representing patriarchal authority in artistic structures that make it seem part of nature at this time. We have already alluded to the interest of James I in political theory. He came to the throne of England with a fully developed patriarchal definition of kingship, one that he published in *The Trew Law of Free Monarchies* (1598) and *The Basilicon Doron* (1599), and in important speeches to Parliament, especially those at the beginning of his reign in 1603 and 1609. Court masques, written by Jonson and others for state occasions, mythologize the Stuart ideology in language echoed by the romances.[4] Although no play can ever be said to have been written for court performance, Shakespeare was, after all, a member of the King's Servants, and both *The Winter's Tale* and *The Tempest* had court performances as part of the celebration for the wedding of Princess Elizabeth and the Elector Palatine. Without sacrificing his independence this most elusive of playwrights might have nevertheless wished to intrigue his royal audience by dealing with themes that interested James, just as we have seen him do in *Measure*.

Several kinds of direct opposition to James also gave rise to increased interest in questions of authority and political theory. Such interest was not new: the last years of Elizabeth's reign, with their worries about the royal subsidy and especially the succession, saw considerable theorizing: "People, we may say, began to speculate about the origin of political authority and the nature of political obligation, about the question as to the ideally best form of government and the question as to where sovereignty lay in England and how much was involved in it."[5] By the second decade of his reign,

James's struggle with Parliament, especially the Puritan sector, had been joined in earnest. This controversy produced the need to make strong claims about the enduring and unchangeable character of the patriarchy.[6] Those grounds lay principally in basing all political authority on nature and the natural power of the father over his children. The latter claim was, of course, not useful during the long reign of Elizabeth, but after 1603 it could again be asserted with gusto. The argument of this chapter is that Shakespeare's romances are part of the political discourse which emerges from this context, and that the plays therefore can be illuminated by being read within its rhetoric.

Nature

Whenever seventeenth-century thinkers reasoned about political authority, they began with nature. It did not matter what their political stripe might be or what conclusions they might lead to, from supporters of divine right to Edward Coke or the Puritans, all appealed first to nature. Hooker began *Of the Laws of Ecclesiastical Polity* (1594) with the Law of Nature and the Law of Scripture, which are harmonious. The Law of Nature determines the position of each creature relative to other creatures in a cosmic order.[7] Bishop Overall's *Convocation Book* (1606) had a formulation that was repeated constantly: "It is also certain that . . . the civil magistrates and their authority continued after the flood for the government of mankind according to the laws of God and nature."[8] James used the phrase frequently: "By the Law of Nature the King becomes a naturall Father to all his Leiges at his Coronation." He reiterated it to Parliament in 1609, "As for the Father of a familie, they had of olde under the Law of Nature *Patriam potestatem,* which was *Potestatem vitae* & *necis,* over their children and family."[9] Richard Mocket, who wrote *God and the King* (1615) at James's request, echoed the commonplace in castigating the Pope: "The Bishop of Rome cannot dispence with the Law of Nature; which *from the first beginning of the reasonable Creature is unchangeable,* nor with the morall Law of God, *whose precepts are indespensable.* But the duty of subiectes in obedience vnto their soveraigne, is grounded upō the law of nature; beginning with our first beginning."[10] Indeed, James's great legal foe, Edward Coke, reasoned from similar premises: "The Law of Nature is that which God at the Time of Creation of the Nature of Man infused into his Heart, for his Preservation and Direction; and this is *Lex Eterna,* the Moral Law, called also the Law of Nature."[11]

Edward Forset, was, however, the master of the correspondence arguments that lay at the heart of theories based in nature, and his *Comparative Discourse of the Bodies Natural and Politique* (1606) laid out one reason for the patriarchalists' great insistence on metaphors such as the body politic: both social inequalities and obedience can easily be demonstrated to be natural. As we remember from *Coriolanus,* no part of the body is allowed, under this way of thought, to disrupt the general operation by asserting its interest against the rest. According to Forset, members of the society correspond to the elements and humors, bound to their duty "where both for comlinesse and use they by natures order placed." Obedience is natural because the ruler is likened to the soul: "as in every man there is both a quickening & ruling soule, and a living and ruled bodie; so in every civill state, there is a directing & commaunding power, & an obeying and subiected allegiance."[12] The patriarchalists dwelt more on natural analogies and correspondences than did their opponents because such thinking carried genetic implications about king and subject that were thought to defeat the growing number of contractualists by implying the unchangeable character of the ruler-subject relationship.[13] The body metaphor made natural and therefore unchangeable the parts of society in their shares, their few rights and many duties, especially obedience in a hierarchical world.

Yet we must recognize that the concept of nature used by the political thinkers quoted above was one of many notions of a richly multivalent term. Lovejoy and Boas summarize the problem with the concept of nature as normative, as a standard for human values:

> Little, indeed, in the history of Western ideas about what is good or bad in conduct, in social and political institutions, and in art, is intelligible without a constant realization of the fact that the sacred word "nature" is probably the most equivocal in the vocabulary of the European people; that the range of connotation of the single term covers conceptions not only distinct but often absolutely antithetic to one another in their implications; and that the writers who have used it have usually been little aware of its equivocality and have at all times tended to slip unconsciously from one of its senses to another.[14]

Readers of *Lear* will have little trouble acknowledging Shakespeare's awareness of the many meanings of *nature,* even if he does not use all sixty-six meanings Lovejoy and Boas record, largely from antique texts. In *The Death of Nature* Carolyn Merchant provides the reader with an excellent analysis of the variations in the meaning of *nature* for the sixteenth and seventeenth centuries. The political theorists quoted above refer to the primary concept of nature as an organic order: "The primary view of nature was the idea that a designed hierarchical order existed in the cosmos and society corresponded to the organic integration of the parts of the body—a projection of the human being onto the cosmos. The term nature comprehended both the innate character and disposition of people and animals and the inherent creative power operating within material objects and phenomena." *Natura naturata* is the instrument of God, her author; she is "a benevolent teacher of the hidden pattern and values God employed in creating the visible cosmos."[15] Since the Fall, however, nature lacks the power to enforce her own laws, which are followed instinctively by all species but humans. They must choose to obey. Secondary grafts on this concept are *natura naturans* and the complex tradition of the pastoral. *Natura naturans* is a creative soul with a will to generate mundane forms. She resembles the Neoplatonic nature in being subordinate only to God and in her superiority to all human artists, who must create according to her laws.[16]

The pastoral tradition, too vast to analyze here in detail, uses the primary image of nature as a setting for human beings, who are in harmony with her, united with her, and respectful of her. The country "provides an appropriate frame for staging a way of life that is 'natural,' *i.e.*, normative."[17] In the pastoral, notions of nature are, by and large, not complex because the mode concentrates on the political and moral consequences of situating humans in a simplified environment for invidious contrast to another setting that is complex and corrupt. The great scope of the mode results from the variety of implications that arise from putting humans in harmony with nature: the variations on notions of simplicity, contentment, and lack of ambition in their contrasts to art, civilization, city, and court can be endlessly woven and rewoven.[18] As we know from *As You Like It* Shakespeare was also fully aware of the variety of pastoral themes, and because pastoral is itself a means of Barthian myth-making, these themes provide Shakespeare with some thematic contradictions of the patriarchal myths in the romances, as we shall see.

The idea of nature as a hierarchical order was essentially conservative: "the interest of the state assumed central importance in comparison to the individual parts."[19] But the sixteenth- and seventeenth-century thinkers magnified the authoritarian aspects of the model, if their works are compared to the *Policraticus* (1159) of John of Salisbury.[20] In *Six Books of the Commonwealth* (1576) Jean Bodin, of whom more later, emphasized the absolute power of the sovereign over all subjects of whatever rank. James I and the writers employed by him asserted the king's absolute authority repeatedly to Parliament and the public. The growth of the nation-state lies behind these claims to aggrandize the head of state at the expense of its body.

Merchant also finds, however, that the organic model of nature supported two contrasting ideas of society: the communal and the utopian. Both challenged the hierarchy. The notion of a rural communal society

> growing out of peasant experience and village culture, was based on the leveling of differences and stressed, instead, the primacy of community, the collective will of the people, and the idea of internal self-regulation and consent. Here the communal whole was still greater and more important than the sum of the parts, but the parts were of equal or nearly equal value. . . . In the communal variant, both the law of God and nature dictated an original equality among the parts of the village community, cooperative land use, and communal sharing of tools and goods.

The utopian tradition was more radical: it presented a vision of "an egalitarian communal society and state of nature like that anticipated during the millennium." This ideal drew on primitive Christianity and looked forward to an era of love and liberty, in which "there would be equal sharing of food, clothing, and property among all people."[21] These ideas were dear to the reformed sects, some of which started experimental communities to anticipate the millenium. The utopian vision echoed the tradition of the Golden Age, and so it was an integral part of the pastoral tradition, whose themes of simplicity, *otium,* and harmony were entirely compatible with the utopian society.[22] These ideas of a political order, which contrast dramatically with the patriarchal, hierarchical order, came to and from Shakespeare in pastoral themes that he could play off against the central myth.

Pericles follows an apparently simple pattern of the romance, where a providential design is fulfilled after long postponement and much distress and where virtues are defined by a series of good and bad examples. Pericles's mission joins the theme of the natural order to the theme of the good ruler: he first travels in quest of a mate to beget successors: "I sought the purchase of a glorious beauty / From whence an issue I might propagate, / Are arms to princes, and bring joys to subjects" (1.2.73–75). The design of the romance, the fulfillment of human wishes after a long suspense,[23] is aptly conveyed by the chivalric device Pericles chooses in the tourney for Thaisa's hand: "his present is / A withered branch, that's only green at top; / The motto, "In hac spe vivo" (2.2.42–44).

The concepts of both nature and the ruler are the old-fashioned Elizabethan notions of a hierarchical order in which fishermen may see the correspondences between fish and humans:

> How from the finny subject of the sea
> These fishers tell the infirmities of men,
> And from their wat'ry empire recollect
> All that may men approve or men detect!
> (2.1.48–51)

The king is an example to his people, and his good or evil will pervade the realm: "It's fit it should be so, for princes are / A model which heaven makes like to itself" (2.2.10–11). The character of the ruler is crucial because, like the green on Pericles's branch, he is at the top and all look to him for hope.

The sea is an excellent vehicle for conveying the relationship between nature and the providential design, for the sea is both powerful and destructive in the short run and beneficent in the long run. It is the medium through which Pericles carries out his patriarchal quest for a family and successors. Sometimes the sea acts as a special providence in washing up Pericles's armor, his heritage from his father, when he needs it for the tournament. The sea twice sends him to his destination: first to Thaisa and later to Marina. The fishermen who learn from the sea to sympathize with their fellow humans help Pericles, giving him garments and hospitality. Yet the storms at sea also protract the fulfillment of human wishes and the providential design, as when Thaisa gives birth to Marina during the storm and the sailors demand that the queen's body be thrown overboard. Ultimately, except for the suffering of Marina and Pericles, the consequences of these events are evaded, but the difference distinguishes providence from simple human wish. Yet at many moments during the action the design of providence seems obscured by the chaos of the elements: "Alas, the seas hath cast me on the rocks" (2.1.5).

Still, it is important for those who would rule and live well to have faith in the design and to respect nature, the normative standard for good action: "Wind, rain, and thunder, remember, earthly man / Is but a substance that must yield to you; / And I, as befits my nature, do obey you" (2.1.2–4). There is sympathy between humans and nature. The tempests of the sea are likened to those within Pericles, and the famine experienced by Tharsus can be our first inkling that Cleon's rule is corrupt. So the play gradually reveals a principle by which those who live in harmony with nature forward the providential design through helping others, following the pattern set by Pericles in sharing nature's bounty with Cleon's starving city. The fishermen, as we have already said, aid Pericles with hospitality as well as repairing his armor. Simonides's court, like the reaches of his kingdom, is a center of hospitality for Pericles even before Thaisa falls in love with him. Cerimon brings Thaisa back to life by following nature's prescriptions. Having been tutored by Marina in right thinking, Lysimachus is quick to help Pericles when he arrives at Mytilene so that the father may recover his daughter.

Evil in *Pericles* is connected to bad relations with women, a theme which fits with Pericles's mission of finding a mate to found a dynasty. The first corrupt relationship is, of course, that of Antiochus and his daughter. Pericles labels their incest "untimely," that is, unnatural. Cleon, the king of Tharsus, is ruled by his wife, Dionyza, in an unnatural subservience. Because Marina puts all young women around her in a shadow, Dionyza arranges her death so that Philoten may prosper in her own right. Worldly competition, which violates gratitude and natural superiority, is the motivation for the attempted murder. The evil couples are linked in their destinies. Both are burned: the first by the act of the gods and the second by revolt of the people. The relationship of Marina to Lysimachus resolves this theme because although Lysimachus comes to the brothel to exploit a prostitute, he is quickly converted by Marina's natural goodness to respect for her:

> For me, be you thoughten
> That I came with no ill intent; for to me
> The very doors and windows savor vilely.
> Fare thee well. Thou art a piece of virtue, and
> I doubt not but thy training hath been noble.
> Hold, here's gold for thee.
> A curse upon him, die he like a thief,
> That robs thee of thy goodness! If thou dost
> Hear from me, it shall be for thy good.
>   (4.6.110–18)

The definition of good rule proceeds, as we have said, by a series of examples through the norms of nature. The untimely relationship of Antiochus to his daughter is contrasted with Simonides's relationship to Thaisa. The first possesses his daughter and kills her suitors; the second entertains them hospitably and gives her freely to the man of her choice, even while mocking the style of the heavy parent. Cleon and Dionyza try to destroy a guest left in their charge and drive a king who has rescued them to despair; Lysimachus immediately helps Pericles and thus brings father and daughter together. Simonides, the model ruler, reminds Pericles of his own father:

> Yon king's to me like to my father's picture,
> Which tells me in that glory once he was;
> Had princes sit like stars about his throne,
> And he the sun for them to reverence;
> None that beheld him but, like lesser lights,
> Did vail their crowns to his supremacy.
>   (2.3.39–44)

The natural imagery reinforces our sense of the correspondences between the political and cosmic orders. Good rulers, moreover, make good followers. Helicanus keeps the nobles of Tyre united and the kingdom stable in Pericles's absence, while both Thaliard and Leonine plan deceit about their orders to commit murder. Furthermore, the conduct of both Marina and Pericles conveys the idea that innate nobility, like evil, will out. When Pericles is the mean stranger at the court of Simonides, the king has little trouble identifying him as someone extraordinary. So Marina quickly appears to Lysimachus, and when she is released from the brothel, she draws around her a group of noble followers to whom she teaches her art that rivals nature:

> Deep clerks she dumbs; and with her neele composes
> Nature's own shape, of bud, bird, branch, or berry,
> That even her art sisters the natural roses;
> Her inkle, silk, twin with the rubied cherry;
> That pupils lacks she none of noble race,
> Who pour their bounty on her; and her gain
> She gives the cursed bawd.
>
> (5.Chorus.5–11)

The hierarchical order of nature supports and ultimately controls the social and political order.

In *Cymbeline* Britain is the swan's nest and the seat of nature, yet the pastoral contrasts in the play are extremely complex. Cymbeline's court is alienated from nature in Britain and Wales and from civilization in Rome. Rome is also contrasted with Italy, the decadent version of civilization, one which corrupts natural values. Cymbeline's tyranny drives from his court the figures of natural nobility who will refresh society at the end because of their experience with contrasting values in different settings. Long before the play opens Cymbeline unjustly banished Belarius, who stole Cymbeline's sons, and together they have created a pastoral counter-court in Wales, from which, as in the Tudor myth, reform will come. While living in a cave, Belarius, Arviragus, and Guiderius have formed a civil society, one that pays respect to place and kind. Arviragus contrasts nature's care of Fidele's grave with "those rich-left heirs that let fathers lie / Without a monument" (4.2.227–28), and Belarius gives Cloten a princely burial, despite his misdeeds: "reverence, / That angel of the world, doth make distinction / Of place 'tween high and low" (4.2.48–50). Arviragus and Guiderius chafe against the limitations of the pastoral life, however, and when Belarius assures them that their life is superior to that at court, the princes remind him that he can compare because he has known both: "We have seen nothing" (3.3.39). Thus Shakespeare prepares us for their military prowess, drawing on the traditional contrast between heroic activity and pastoral *otium*.

Cymbeline also banishes Posthumus, who is corrupted by Italy into losing faith in Imogen. Just as Belarius is a double for Cymbeline, so the play develops through a series of doubles for Posthumus. The first is the oafish Cloten, preoccupied with rank and clothing, who with his mother dominates Cymbeline's court. Having aspired to Imogen's hand, Cloten continues to woo her and acts out Posthumus's misogynistic rage in determining to rape her while wearing Posthumus's clothing.[24] Because he is a parody of a courtier, Cloten is appropriately killed by Guiderius. Italy offers a second double: Iachimo, who would ruin Posthumus's marriage on a wager. Iachimo's baroque language during his adventure in Imogen's chamber marks him as effete and artificial in the pejorative sense.[25] As soon as Posthumus returns to Britain and suits himself like a British peasant, he defeats Iachimo: "so I fight / Against the part I came with" (5.1.24–25). Iachimo believes the air in Britain has made him feeble because he has been bested by such a low-born person. The third double is Lucius, the valiant and honorable leader of the Roman troops in Britain, who befriends Imogen, pleads for her to Cymbeline, seems betrayed by her, but is ultimately saved. His generous and forgiving spirit needs to be regained by both Posthumus and Cymbeline.

Those who behave according to nature further the providential design contained in the oracle from Jupiter: "When as a lion's whelp shall, to himself unknown, without seeking find, and be embrac'd by a piece of tender air; and when from a stately cedar shall be lopp'd branches, which, being dead many years, shall after revive, be jointed to the old stock, and freshly grow; then shall Posthumus end his miseries, Britain be fortunate and flourish in peace and plenty" (5.5.438–44). The natural imagery suggests the harmony between providence and nature. Without looking for them, Imogen finds her brothers, who kill Cloten and with Posthumus assert Britain's freedom by defeating Rome. As Cymbeline makes peace with Rome, Britain seems a fortunate island indeed. When Cymbeline has lost his corrupting step-family and regained the one identified with nature, he can abandon tyranny and forgive Belarius. The patriarchy, which has tottered, is firmly reestablished with successors; Cymbeline becomes the radiant sun in the west united with the Roman eagle of imperial Caesar.

As in *Pericles*, in *Cymbeline* relations to women are a code for evil. Again an ambitious mother dominates a weak ruler: wanting the succession for Cloten, the Queen first hopes for his marriage to Imogen, then failing that, plots Imogen's death. The relations of Imogen to Posthumus, Cymbeline, Cloten, and Iachimo serve to depoliticize the action so that when she regains father (really a second in Belarius), husband, and brothers, the drama seems complete. It is, however, the historical fate of Britain to which we return at the end. The relation of the ruler to nature in *Cymbeline* is made problematic by the fact that he begins the action as a tyrant and learns how to rule well by valuing those who live in harmony with nature. Yet Shakespeare's dramatic technique makes the change relatively easy to manage: the deaths of the Queen and Cloten free Cymbeline to accept the influence of Imogen, as signalled by their long conversation in the court scene, as well Belarius and the princes. In *The Winter's Tale*, because Leontes's tyranny is self-engendered, this process, like everything else in the play, is more complex.

Possibly because *The Winter's Tale* is based on romance
rather than history, its patriarchal elements seem more
strongly depoliticized by nature. Here nature comprehends
rather than simplifies. As the title suggests, *The Winter's Tale*
deals with time, with living according to the seasons, and with
death, not only as an event, but as a theme. Father Time
appears to provide the audience with a sense of the order
that lies behind all other orders:

> Let me pass
> The same I am, ere ancient'st order was
> Or what is now receiv'd. I witness to
> The times that brought them in; so shall I do
> To th' freshest things now reigning, and make stale
> The glistering of this present, as my tale
> Now seems to it.
>
> (4.1.9–15)

The process by which the aging winter characters try to assure their succession by progeny is the overarching action of
the drama, joining the two parts of the play and implied by
the oracle. The sheepshearing festival, a seasonal event,
makes natural the link between sexuality and death, where
lovemaking will give progeny to compensate for the death of
a generation.[26] Perdita's flower speech rehearses the seasons,
assigning flowers to each age, and then connecting sex to
death:

> pale primroses,
> That die unmarried, ere they can behold
> Bright Phoebus in his strength—a malady
> Most incident to maids; bold oxlips and
> The crown imperial; lillies of all kinds,
> The flow'r-de-luce being one. O, these I lack,
> To make you garlands of, and my sweet friend,
> To strew him o'er and o'er!
> *Florizel*   What, like a corse?
> *Perdita* No, like a bank for love to lie and play on,
>   Not like a corse; or if, not to be buried,
>   But quick and in mine arms.
>
> (4.4.122–32)

Florizel's reaction to Perdita's ceremony is to interfere with time, to freeze it at one sublime moment: "When you speak, sweet, / I'd have you do it ever" (4.4.136–37). But the play insists such immortal longings cannot be fulfilled within nature: instead time offers not the frozen eternity of the grecian urn but the substitution of one nightingale for another or a Florizel for a Mamillius. Mutability is nature's eternal pattern in which one of a species succeeds another, keeping the kind alive.

The nature of *The Winter's Tale* is *natura naturans,* great creating nature, a source of fertility to which all other forms of creativity are subservient. Thus, the fertility of women is emphasized. Hermione begins the play spread to a goodly bulk, and Paulina is the mother of three daughters. Sexuality is more prominent here than in the other romances. The shepherd thinks Perdita may be the result of backstairs work and that all youths should sleep out the ages between ten and twenty-three (presumably when they would marry). Autolycus's songs and banter are full of "blood" and tumbling in the hay. *Natura naturans* as the creator of mundane forms is the subject of debate between Polixenes and Perdita, who refuses to grow gillyvors because they are nature's bastards. Perdita likens the art by which humans produce grafts to women's painting, artifice that distorts nature. Polixenes's reply is that because all art works according to nature's rules, nature herself has created the graft. In *The Winter's Tale*, then, nature is the basis of everything humans create.

The open hospitality of the shepherds during the festival, in which the old shepherd urges Perdita to emulate the warmth and geniality of his lost wife, is a contrast both to the hostile atmosphere at Leontes's court and to Polixenes's spying on his son. The rulers of Sicilia and Bohemia need to regain their faith in their human ties before they can achieve the poise of the shepherd. The faith which Leontes and Polixenes must gain is simple yet mystified by the scene with the statue, which is presented as a miracle. Does faith bring the statue to life? Does the life which the statue represents bring faith? The important outcomes have been predicted by the oracle, to which Paulina holds Leontes's allegiance. Ultimately, one feels a trust in natural processes because they prove socially acceptable: although Florizel rebels against his father and woos a shepherd girl, he has chosen a princess. Even though Perdita fears retribution because she has accepted a prince, she is socially worthy of him: "Our King, being ready to leap out of himself for joy of his found daughter, as if that joy were now become a loss, cries, 'O, thy mother, thy mother!' then asks Bohemia forgiveness; then embraces his son-in-law; then again worries he his daughter with clipping her; now he thanks the old shepherd, which stands by like a weather-bitten conduit of many kings' reigns" (5.2.50–57). If one attempts to subvert these processes, as does Leontes in having Perdita destroyed, nature protects the babe in killing Antigonus, who should preside over her death, and nature also provides the shepherd to care for her until her place in the social order is secure.

After Florizel and Perdita appear at Leontes's court, the audience knows that nature may be trusted and is therefore worthy of the faith Leontes must place in the statue to believe that Hermione lives. Polixenes has a lesser task: he need only accept a highly desirable relationship, apologize, and forgive—in short, he too must learn to trust others. We now understand why Paulina puts both kings to the test of the statue: are they trusting enough to accept her mysterious ways of bringing the statue to life? Will they set their own judgments above those more in touch with nature's ways? Both prove to have given up tyranny for a better, albeit mysterious, order.

As do *Pericles* and *Cymbeline*, *The Winter's Tale* depoliticizes its patriarchal structures by presenting its conflicts in sexual relationships, in terms of infidelity and marriage choice. Although women are no longer a source of evil, relations to them define the tyranny of both kings. Leontes's destruction of his family is identical with his misrule; Polixenes blames Perdita for Florizel's rebellion against him. Both kings seek to dominate those on whom they utterly depend, and the oracle makes clear, where the political and the personal are indistinguishable, the crucial problem for both kings: heirs.

New Definitions

To understand *The Tempest* new definitions of nature are necessary. Prospero's magic, the witchcraft of Sycorax, and the bestiality of Caliban assume a Neoplatonic universe that was described for the sixteenth century by three major works: Ficino's *De vita coelitus comparanda* (1489), Agrippa's *De occulta philosophia libri tres* (1531), and Della Porta's *Magiae naturalis libri viginti* (1589).[27] The Neoplatonic universe was a hierarchy extending from base earth to the divine intellect. All life was made up of body, soul, and spirit; corporeal objects were imperfect copies, in the world's body, of the pure Ideas in the divine mind. The soul of the world was everywhere and contained celestial images of the divine Ideas. "Linking the celestial images in the world soul to the matter in the body was the world spirit. The *spiritus mundi* was the vehicle by which the influences of superior powers in the celestial realm could be brought down and joined to the inferior powers in the terrestrial region. At the basis of Neoplatonic hierarchical magic, therefore, was a causal chain linking elemental and celestial objects and making it possible for bodies above the terrestrial sphere to affect and alter those on earth."[28] The magus could use the causal chain to employ celestial powers in marrying superiors to inferiors. Thus, could he manipulate and control nature in specific instances. So Prospero employs superior powers to control those inferior, while Caliban represents the Platonic disdain for matter, a source of disorder, a thing of darkness. Sycorax, the witch, has her magic too, but it is limited to the use of devils and can only partially control lower forms of spirits.[29] Prospero reminds Ariel that Sycorax could not undo the spell by which she bound him in a tree: "it was a torment / To lay upon the damn'd, which Sycorax / Could not again undo: it was mine Art, / When I arriv'd and heard thee, that made gape / The pine, and let thee out" (1.2.289–93). And so the play turns on a contest for the bare island between two kinds of magic: the witchcraft of Sycorax and the primitive life of her son Caliban contend with the magic of the colonist Prospero, who possesses a greater art that summons powers unknown to the witch and justifies his conquest of the island by moral superiority over the savage:

> This island's mine, by Sycorax my mother,
> Which thou tak'st from me. When thou cam'st first,
> Thou strok'st me and mad'st much of me, wouldst give
>   me
> Water with berries in't, and teach me how
> To name the bigger light, and how the less,
> That burn by day and night; and then I lov'd thee
> And show'd thee all the qualities o' th' isle,
> The fresh springs, brine-pits, barren land and fertile.
>
> . . . .
>
> For I am all the subjects that you have,
> Which first was mine own king; and here you sty me
> In this hard rock, whiles you do keep from me
> The rest o' th' island.
> *Prospero*   Thou most lying slave,
> Whom stripes may move, not kindness! I have us'd thee,
> Filth as thou art, with humane care, and lodg'd thee
> In mine own cell, till thou didst seek to violate
> The honor of my child.
>
> (1.2.333–50)

From the perspective of this contrast it seems clear that *The Tempest* is not a pastoral play, although it does employ pastoral themes. The tempest, usually providential, is the work of man. The island is not a normative setting with which humans live in harmony.[30] Instead it becomes a mirror in which each temperament sees itself. For the good Gonzalo the island is green and lush; for some of his shipmates it is desert and uninhabitable; for Antonio it is tawny. As the ship's party gradually reacts to its surroundings and predicament, it becomes clear that *The Tempest* is more a play about the power of the human imagination than about the human response to nature. The island is not efficacious; the play instead shows Prospero using it for his purposes. Only Caliban knows its beauties, and they are lost on Stephano and Trinculo. The lovers do not find each other in the pastoral way, but are brought together by Prospero and rigorously controlled. The island does not inspire contentment. Instead each group brings its ambitions for rule to the island, and only Gonzalo's is a genuine fantasy. He would be a king to make the island an ideal commonwealth, of which more below. But Sebastian and Antonio hope to exploit the death of Ferdinand and the isolation of Claribel to make Sebastian ruler of Naples, while Stephano dreams of making the island itself his kingdom and replacing Prospero as Caliban's master.

In a pastoral the withdrawal of characters to a simplified, natural setting changes them, and they return to society with values clarified.[31] Because nature cannot offer that process here, Prospero replaces it with his own: an imaginative reenactment of the sufferings visited upon him, a pseudorevenge. Prospero himself thus replaces the Providence Divine he tells Miranda brought them to the island. Through the use of Ariel as harpy, Prospero pretends that providential nature is punishing Alonso, Sebastian, and Antonio:

> You are three men of sin, whom Destiny,
> That hath to instrument this lower world
> And what is in't, the never-surfeited sea
> Hath caus'd to belch you up, and on this island
> Where man doth not inhabit—you 'mongst men
> Being most unfit to live. . . .
> .   .   .   .
>   But remember—
> For that's my business to you—that you three
> From Milan did supplant good Prospero;
> Expos'd unto the sea, which hath requit it,
> Him and his innocent child; for which foul deed
> The pow'rs, delaying, not forgetting, have
> Incens'd the seas and shores, yea, all the creatures,
> Against your peace.
>
>   (3.3.52–75)

Ferdinand invokes the same idea when he says of Miranda, "by immortal Providence she's mine" (5.1.189), when we know that Prospero has arranged their wedding. Yet the irony of *The Tempest* is that this familiar myth of the romance does not work: Antonio is almost entirely silent after Prospero reveals himself; Stephano is still drunk; only Caliban seems to have learned from his experience: "What a thrice-double ass / Was I to take this drunkard for a god / And worship this dull fool!" (5.1.299–301).

By putting Prospero in total control of the island, Shakespeare exposes the Barthian myth-making of the earlier romances. We see in Ferdinand's exclamation and in Prospero's use of a seemingly providential nature for his own purposes the need to claim that a natural order lies at the bottom of human power structures. The fact that the lowest orders of nature are vile justifies their being controlled by the noble, but that seems possible only on the island: Stephano and Antonio give no assurance that back in Italy they will not again threaten authority; nor do we have any clear sense that Antonio has ruled badly in Milan or that he may not have been preferable to Prospero as ruler. Instead the play acknowledges that its fantasy of power has been just that and must be relinquished for the contingent, ambiguous power of the real world, that Prospero's possession of the island is but an elegant version of the dreams of Stephano and Sebastian.

The two loci of nature poetry in *The Tempest* are the wedding masque and Prospero's abjuration of his magic: both represent a kind of nature seen nowhere else in the play.[32] The masque celebrates the fertility of nature as a setting for the hopes of issue from a blessed marriage, but the social order is not, even here, in harmony with nature. Ceres cannot abide Venus and Cupid, and so they do not appear. Sexuality is banished, while the union is blessed by the matronly Juno. The harvesters' holiday dance is interrupted by Prospero's thought of the conspiracy against him. When Prospero evokes the nature over which he has had magical dominion, the effect is not to describe a natural setting, but to pay tribute to the enormous power he has enjoyed through the command of natural forces, quite a different thing from living in harmony with nature:

> I have bedimm'd
> The noontide sun, call'd forth the mutinous winds,
> And 'twixt the green sea and the azur'd vault
> Set roaring war; to the dread rattling thunder
> Have I given fire, and rifted Jove's stout oak
> With his own bolt; the strong-bas'd promontory
> Have I made shake, and by the spurs pluck'd up
> The pine and cedar.
>
> (5.1.41–48)

This "fantasy of omnipotence"[33] gained through his learning drew Prospero away from genuine political power once, and it must be abjured before he can resume his dukedom.

Natural Nobility

The gospel, said the Puritan royalist William Perkins, did not do away with the law of nature which establishes inequality: "In a commonwealth all must not be equal; but some above, some under others with regard to wealth, and therefore such as have sundry forms . . . may lawfully enjoy them."[34] In this assertion Perkins echoed those of Forset, Hooker, and countless earlier thinkers about the order of nature. That Shakespeare's England was a social hierarchy is hardly a secret, but the social mobility,[35] especially into the gentle class, and James's freedom in dispensing noble titles increased concern about cheapening true nobility. In *The Book of Honour* (1625), Francis Markham said that as titles multiply, those that are most ancient lend credibility and value to the rest.[36] Forty years before, Sir Thomas Smith began his chapter on gentlemen with the statement, "Gentlemen be those whom their blood and race make noble and knowne." Smith believed that ancient lineage would produce virtuous and noble progeny because such children would enjoy advantages in a great family, but because a generation might also fail to produce successors, the king should recognize virtue in creating new nobility.[37]

Mervyn James's fascinating study of Stuart society in the Durham region provides insight into how the noble elite of the north, largely recusant Catholic, came to worship their ancient lineage as their daughters married heirs of coal-mining fortunes from Newcastle.[38] As a consequence of the growing number of fresh titles and the increased wealth of those below noble status, nobility of birth was gradually stressed in the courtesy books, written to define the gentleman. In the model of them all, Castiglione's *Courtier* (1528), the courtier benefits from noble birth, but it is not required for the status,[39] a sentiment echoed by Sir Thomas Elyot.[40] By 1563, however, Lawrence Humphrey was insisting on the importance of birth to a nobleman: "commonly the childe expresseth his sire, and posterity (if not changeling) covets the steps of the ancestors."[41] In the courtesy books, the same attitude gradually emerged: "As class lines harden with the soberer times that James I ushered in, the requirement of birth becomes more stressed."[42] Art represents this value by mystifying genealogy.[43]

Edmund Spenser provided Shakespeare with a model for representing the value of birth or bloodline, what Kermode calls the "magic of nobility."[44] In Book VI of *The Fairie Queen*, both Pastorella and the Salvage Man are of noble birth, but they grow up in nature. Their conduct, without the advantages that Humphrey and Smith acknowledge, is unmistakable evidence that blood will tell:

> O what an easie thing is to descry
> The gentle bloud, how euer it be wrapt
> In sad misfortunes foul deformity,
> And wretched sorrowes, which haue often hapt?
> For howsoever it may grow mis-shapt.
> Like this wyld man, being vndisciplynd,
> That to all vertuw it may seeme unapt,
> Yet will it shew some sparkes of gentle mynd,
> And at the last breake forth in his owne proper kynd.[45]

The Salvage Man cannot talk, but he tenderly cares for Serena, who has been wounded by the Blatant Beast, until Arthur and Timias arrive; then he disappears with his noble blood. Pastorella is like Perdita in that she is royally born, but raised by the shepherd Meliboe. Calidore, like Florizel, disguises himself as a shepherd to woo Pastorella, who is reunited with her long-lost mother in a moving episode:

> Who euer is the mother of one chylde,
> Which hauing thought long dead, she fyndes aliue,
> Let her by proofe of that, which she hath fylde
> In her own breast, this mothers ioy descriue:
> For other none such passion con contriue
> In perfect forme, as this good Lady felt,
> When she so faire a daughter saw suruiue,
> As *Pastorella* was, that nigh she swelt
> For passing joy, which did all into pitty melt.
>
> (6.12.21)

This could well be a description of Hermione in her reunion with Perdita. As Perdita's severest critic, Polixenes, describes her, "Nothing she does or seems / But smacks of some thing greater than herself, / Too noble for this place" (4.4.157–59). Perdita does nothing to promote her rise in society. In fact, she is more conservative socially than Florizel. When Polixenes expresses his rage at their relationship, Perdita scolds her lover, "How often have I told you 'twould be thus! / How often said, my dignity would last / But till 'twere known!" (4.4.475–77). Florizel's unwavering faith in the fact that he and Perdita are meant for one another transforms rebellion into a comfortable reassertion of the patriarchal order. Blood royal will recognize itself anywhere.

Imogen's brothers' dislike of their primitive life may help the audience expect them to rise to the opportunities presented them in Cloten's appearance and in the battle of the narrow pass. Although Belarius has given them a good education, telling them stories like those in *The Fairie Queen,* their heroism in battle and their sensitivity clearly derive from their royal blood:

> 'Tis wonder
> That an invisible instinct should frame them
> To royalty unlearn'd, honour untaught,
> Civility not seen from other, valor
> That wildly grows in them but yields a crop
> As if it had been sow'd.
>
> (4.2.177–82)

We have already noted similar effects in *Pericles* where both Pericles and Marina are quickly identified as suitable mates by Thaisa and Lysimachus. The latter is made cautious by Marina's unconventional surroundings, but still he declares, "She's such a one that, were I well assur'd / Came of a gentle kind and noble stock, / I'd wish no better choice, and think me rarely wed" (5.1.70–72). When royal lovers follow their instincts to socially acceptable mates and when natural nobility is so apparent to all beholders, the audience can hardly escape the impression that nature accords with the social order.

Contradictions

The same social mobility which caused anxiety about nobility supplied Shakespeare with elements within his plays that contradict their patriarchal myths. To these he added pastoral themes which function in a similar way, allowing the audience a subversive perspective on the central power structure. Although they may allow an audience a greater awareness of the central myth, contradictions hardly destroy it. Instead they may sustain power structures by admitting their ambiguity and by making them seem invulnerable to difference: "There can be no such thing as an unambiguous expression of power, for it is precisely in ambiguity that power resides, making it as capable of direct as of indirect action."[46] Contradictions alert an audience, however, to the fact that power relationships represented in a given work are not so innocent as they may seem. The most striking instance occurs in *The Winter's Tale* where Perdita's foster family ends the play as gentlemen in Leontes's court. This seems a kindly parody of a trend toward regentrification of the country and immigation to London in Jacobean England. To understand why the process occurred we should recall the population explosion described in Chapter Two. As a result of that increase in people the cities had severe social problems and the country prospered. In 1577 William Harrison described the improvement of country life in three terms which old men recognize: "a multitude of chimneys lately erected"; "the great (although not general) amendment of lodging"; and "the exchange of vessel, as of treen platters into pewter."[47] This prosperity, historians tell us, came from the rise in population, as increased food prices profited the farmers in a favorable balance of trade with London. In her study of the English yeomen Mildred Campbell shows how they profited more than they were hurt by the price revolution; they grew their food and raised sheep for clothing: "Hence the rise in the prices of these staples affected their expense outlay to a much less degree than it augmented their incomes which were based almost wholly upon the sale of grain, wool, and livestock."[48]

The great number of chimneys noted by Harrison's old men were in fact a substantial, and lasting, mirror of the prosperity of the country. The phenomenon has been described as "the rebuilding of rural England, 1570–1640":[49] "For every grand new house built by a Cecil or a Howard there were dozens of solid farmhouses of the upper yeomanry or gentry built or improved. New cottages testified to the rising rural population; but bigger and better farmhouses and country seats, whether the stone buildings of the Cotswolds or the timber-framed and pargeted houses of Suffolk, meant more money."[50] Harrison's description of how much money and the things it bought is quite vivid:

> although peradventure four pounds of old rent be improved to forty, fifty or a hundred pounds, yet will the farmer, as another palm or date tree, think his gains very small toward the end of his term if he have not six or seven years' rent lying by him, therewith to purchase a new lease, beside a fair gar-

nish of pewter on his cupboard, with so much more in odd
vessel going about the house, three or four feather beds, so
many coverlids and carpets of tapestry, a silver salt, a bowl for
wine (if not a whole neast), and a dozen of spoons to furnish
up the suit.[51]

Francis Bacon saw the commons who work their own
land as the defense of the realm. England should "breed a
subject to live in convenient plenty and no servile condition,
and to keep the plough in the hands of the owners, and not
mere hirelings. And thus indeed you shall attain to Virgil's
character which he gives to ancient Italy: *Terra potens armis
Atque ubere glebae*."[52] In 1608 John Fletcher attributed the
failure of his pastoral play, *The Faithful Shepherdess*, to the fact
that his audience did not know he was representing shepherds in the tradition Bacon described. Fletcher accused his
audience of expecting "a play of country hired Shepherds, in
gray cloakes, with curtaild dogs in strings, sometimes laughing together, and sometimes killing one another." His shepherds, Fletcher said, are of a better class, the type that Virgil
spoke: "But you are ever to remember Shepherds to be such,
as all the ancient Poets and moderne of understanding have
received them: that is, the owners of flockes and not hyer-
lings."[53] Both Bacon and Fletcher were idealizing complex
situations, for most English farmers did not own their land
nor shepherds their sheep, but a respect for the wealth of the
country and the dignity it brings, sanctioned by the ancients,
is common to their attitudes. In *The State of England 1600*, Sir
Thomas Wilson supplied a clue to these attitudes as he described a process of regentrification of the country and of
sons of yeomen becoming gentlemen:

> It cannot be denied but the common people are very rich,
> albeit they be much decayed from the states they were wont to
> have, for the gentlemen, which were wont to addict them-
> selves to the wars, are now for the most part grown to become
> good husbands and know as well how to improve their lands
> to the uttermost as the farmer or countryman, so that they
> take their farms into their hands as the leases expire, and

either till themselves or else let them out to those who will give the most. . . . the yeomanry of England is decayed and become servants to gentlemen, which were wont to be the glory of the country and good neighbourhood and hospitality . . . but my young masters the sons of such, not contented with the states of their fathers to be counted yeoman and called John or Robert (such an one), but must skip into his velvet breeches and silken doublet and, getting to be admitted into some Inn of Court or Chancery, must ever after think scorn to be called any other than gentlemen; which gentlemen indeed, perceiving them unfit to do them that service that their fathers did, when their leases do expire, turn them out of their lands.[54]

The old shepherd in *The Winter's Tale* is, as we have said, very like Wilson's and Campbell's yeoman in being the soul of hospitality during the sheepshearing. This communal life with its leveling and mixing of classes forms a social contrast to the court: it is an alternative kind of society which is also natural. Florizel likens the festival to a meeting of the petty gods, little knowing that his father and Camillo are part of the throng. The entire hierarchy of the society is present, with the old shepherd in charge; the disguises obliterate social distinctions; Dorcas, Mopsa, and Autolycus jostle the dancers who performed the Twelve Satyrs before the king. (This seems literally true: this dance is the antimasque from *Oberon*.[55]) Polixenes intrudes the royal imperatives into this setting and makes the contrast between the two societies overt, but very much at his own expense, for he plays the tyrant and risks losing an heir. Shakespeare does not attempt to resolve the contrast between the two societies: they simply coexist as they did historically.

When the old shepherd and his son accompany Florizel and Perdita to Leontes's court, the shepherd's son, like Wilson's young masters, becomes a gentleman. This social mobility is a clear contradiction of the natural nobility described above. Both concepts were part of Shakespeare's world, but he makes them collide in the same family so that the audience can see the conflict: "But I was a gentleman born before my father; for the King's son took me by the

hand, and call'd me brother; and then the two kings call'd my
father brother; and then the Prince my brother and the Princess my sister call'd my father father; and so we wept, and
there was the first gentleman-like tears that ever we shed"
(5.2.140–46).

In *Pericles* Boult performs a similar function, showing the
audience not just the moral issue of prostitution which concerns Marina, but the economics of the bawdy house as well.
The Bawd instructs Boult to deflower Marina because she is
chasing customers away from the brothel: "She's able to
freeze the god Priapus, and undo a whole generation" (4.6.3–
4). After Marina has inspired Lysimachus to reform and
Lysimachus curses Boult, the doorkeeper is even more determined to "crack the glass of her virginity, and make the rest
malleable," not because of lust but because of income. The
confrontation between them has little to do with Gower's old
story and much to do with the economic exploitation of prostitution and the degradation of the poor. Their exchange
contradicts the moral simplicity of the rest of the action:

> Thou hold'st a place for which the pained'st fiend
> Of hell would not in reputation change.
> Thou art the damned doorkeeper to every
> Coistrel that comes inquiring for his Tib.
> To the choleric fisting of every rogue
> Thy ear is liable; thy food is such
> As hath been belch'd on by infected lungs.
> *Boult* What would you have me do? Go to the wars, would
> you? Where a man may serve seven years for the loss of
> a leg, and have not money enough in the end to buy
> him a wooden one?
> *Marina* Do anthing but this thou doest. Empty
> Old receptacles, or common shores, of filth;
> Serve by indenture to the common hangman.
>   (4.6.164–77)

Fortunately Lysimachus has given Marina enough money to
buy Boult off until she can earn her way, but the arts by
which she attracts her noble pupils to her come from another

kind of story in which money is called "bounty." The entire
brothel sequence is conducted in terms of money, which is
hardly mentioned elsewhere in the play, where Marina's noble pupils provide her "bounty" (nature's word) to continue
to pay the bawd.

Cymbeline and *The Tempest* use pastoral themes to disrupt
their patriarchal structures. Although the critical attitudes of
Imogen's brothers toward being raised in a Welsh cave are
necessary to their emergence as heroes in the war against
Rome, their indictment almost destroys the pastoral effect.
The themes of contentment and harmony that Belarius artic-
ulates mean little to these vigorous young men who have only
Belarius's doctrine to balance their sense of confinement:

> Out of your proof you speak. We poor unfledg'd
> Have never wing'd from view o' th' nest, nor know not
> What air's from home. Hap'ly this life is best,
> If quiet life be best, sweeter to you
> That have a sharper known, well corresponding
> With your stiff age; but unto us it is
> A cell of ignorance, traveling abed
> A prison, or a debtor that not dares
> To stride a limit.
> *Arviragus* What should we speak of
> When we are old as you? When we shall hear
> The rain and wind beat dark December, how,
> In this our pinching cave, shall we discourse
> The freezing hours away? We have seen nothing.
> We are beastly, subtle as the fox for prey,
> Like warlike as the wolf for what we eat;
> Our valor is to chase what flies. Our cage
> We make a choir, as doth the prison's bird,
> And sing our bondage freely.
>
> (3.3.27–44)

Relief comes when Imogen soon appears at their cave and
the war with Rome liberates them to take part in heroic action. Yet their criticism makes the pastoral life seem empty
and meaningless, more a rejection of the court by Belarius

than a source of contentment and harmony. This sense seriously threatens our idea that Britain is reformed by those close to nature.

In *The Tempest* the countrapuntal effect is more complex because the pastoral themes are implicitly contrasted with Prospero's rule. The island, like More's Utopia, tempts us to look for an ideal commonwealth of the kind Gonzalo describes, which in the utopian pastoral tradition is an egalitarian, communistic society in which property, law, and work are needless because nature provides a sufficiency for all:

> I' th' commonwealth I would by contraries
> Execute all things; for no kind of traffic
> Would I admit; no name of magistrate;
> Letters should not be known; riches, poverty,
> And use of service, none; contract, succession,
> Bourn, bound of land, tilth, vineyard, none;
> No use of metal, corn, or wine, or oil
> No occupation; all men idle, all,
> And women too, but innocent and pure;
> No sovereignty—
> *Sebastian* Yet he would be king on't.
> *Antonio* The latter end of his commonwealth forgets the
> beginning.
> *Gonzalo* All things in common nature should produce
> Without sweat or endeavor. Treason, felony,
> Sword, pike, knife, gun, or need of any engine,
> Would I not have; but nature should bring forth,
> Of it own kind, all foison, all abundance,
> To feed my innocent people.
>
>   (2.1.149–66)

The problem with Gonzalo's vision is not the mockery of his companions, but the fact that he who would have no magistrate or sovereign would be a king.[56] Like Prospero, Gonzalo cannot imagine a society without a king. His utopian dream illustrates how fixed the most altruistic of us are in our cultural codes. So the contradiction between Gonzalo's commonwealth and the role of its author extends to Prospero's island, which might be a utopia, but is a petty kingdom with an authoritarian ruler of three subjects—a spirit, a daughter, and a monster, two of whom want their freedom. It is no utopia nor was it meant to be. Sebastian and Antonio know that they, no more than Caliban, could live without law and work. Their natures, not Gonzalo's, make his ideal state impossible, but it stands as a traditional ideal society to show the audience all that Prospero's island kingdom is not.

Family

The authority of the patriarchal ruler comes from the family, from the biblical injunction to honor father and mother. Obedience to parents is extended to all superiors, as in Thomas Becon's *Catechisme:* "Our schoolmaster, and also our catechist, taught us that this commandment of God doth not only require of us honour and obedience toward our fathers and mothers, but also toward the temporal magistrates, and the ministers of God's word, and toward our elders and all such as be our superiours and governors."[57] A description of the tradition that lies behind this thinking is beyond our scope, but it is important to understand why patriarchal political theories suddenly emerge in seventeenth-century England: "What happened, very simply, was that the contractual theory of political obligation—with its insistence that the political order was conventional as demonstrated by its origins—contradicted the traditional view that human relationships were the natural outgrowths of the familial association and its paternal authority. The patriarchal doctrine, in response, was transformed from a vaguely articulated societal theory into an intentional political ideology."[58] For sophisticated theorists like Bodin, the father's authority in the family is "the true modell for the government of a Commonweale."[59] Bodin does not identify the father's power with that of the ruler, but as the century wore on, pressure from other theorists led the patriarchalists to become more urgent than logical in their representations of the father's power until Robert Filmer in *Patriarcha* (c. 1640) traced the king's absolute authority back to Adam as the first father.[60] In response to the consent theorists, then, patriarchalists held that the political order was not just analogous to, but identical with the family order, that the commonwealth was simply a large and complex household, that political authority, as we have seen, was natural, not, as the consentualists would have it, conventional. What men had not created, they could not change. In their elaboration of these ideas the patriarchal writers were using such commonplace terms that the consentualists employed them too. In defending the contract theory, Thomas Bilson still used the familiar language: "The Prince hath the same charge in the commonwealth that everie private man hath in his familie."[61] In explaining the emergence of a patriarchal ideology in England after 1603, we also need to remember that a father succeeded a virgin queen on the throne of England. As Schochet says, if in the sixteenth century patriarchalism had been "more than a burgeoning concept,"[62] it would surely have proved an embarrassment to defenders of the several Renaissance female rulers. But when James came to England, the moment for the theory came with him.

The importance of the family in Reformation thought should also not be underestimated. Fatherhood was "transformed into a religious office, with its duties and its obligations prescribed by the Word."[63] England was therefore full of books about the right ordering of a household, like Perkins's *Christian Oeconomie* (1609) in which we read, "The *good man or master of the familie,* is a person, in whom resteth the private and proper government of the whole houshold, and he comes not unto it by election, as it falleth out in other states, but by the ordinance of God, setled even in the order of nature."[64] By fusing the concepts of the state and society, the patriarchalists made obedience to the sovereign as natural and unquestionable as obeying one's father. So the patriarchal ideology was transparently natural.

It is important to distinguish between the relation of man to wife and father to child in this political theory. If we look at the two great continental political theorists who base political authority on the family, Althusius[65] and Bodin, for how they describe the power of the *paterfamilias,* we find that both stress the subservience of the wife to her husband and that her obedience comes as a result of a lawful contract while the power of the father over his children is natural. Bodin reviews the history of marriage relationships, including a debate about divorce in various cultures, before concluding that the wife's subjection to her husband accords with "the lawes both of God and man." His next chapter deals with children and bears the significant gloss: "The power of the Father over his children is the onely naturall power."[66]

In the context of these ideas, the exclusion of the mother from many of Shakespeare's plays which deal centrally with power—*Henry IV, Lear, The Tempest*—may be no accident. Certainly her invisibility eliminates the necessity of dealing with the obedience to the mother to which the Bible also enjoins children. When Francis Bacon created an ideal patriarchal society in his *New Atlantis* (1627), he also made the mother invisible, but less gracefully than Shakespeare, for Bacon reminds the reader of her exclusion. In this society obedience to the father is enforced by the governor: "The governor assisteth, to the end to put in execution by his public authority the decrees and orders of the Tirsan [father], if they should be disobeyed, though that seldom needeth, such reverence and obedience they give to the order of nature." In the Feast of the Family, which is celebrated by the patriarch and children at the state's expense, the father is attended by both sons and daughters, "and if there be a mother from whose body the whole lineage is descended, there is a traverse placed in a loft above on the right hand of the chair [of the father], with a privy door and a carved window of glass, leaded with gold and blue, where she sitteth, but is not seen." The king is acknowledged to be in the father's debt for his propagation of subjects, and during the ceremony hymns are sung to Adam, Noah, Abraham, and in praise of Christ's birth. About this feast Bacon's narrator concludes, "I have never heard of a solemnity wherein nature did so much preside."[67] Here, as in the family portraits Goldberg analyzes, human fecundity is idealized, but the important relationship lies between father and child. By rendering the wife-mother invisible, both Bacon and Shakespeare represent a patriarch who "absorbs female creativity."[68]

We should understand that the father of the political theorists had little to do with the realities of fatherhood in seventeenth-century England or France.[69] As Hinton suggests, "The family provided them with an insight into what seemed to them to be real and natural in political relationships, in contrast to the artificiality of man-made regulations. . . . Husbands and fathers owed their popularity with the thinkers entirely to their suitability as vehicles for argument in the world of ideas; they were devices for the logical deployment of thoughts that in themselves owed nothing to the actual state of affairs in real families."[70] Because the patriarchal theorists were conservative, they sought in fact to restore lost authority to the father. Like James, Bodin would give back to the father the power of life and death over his children, a power antique Romans had and gave up during the decadence. James, as we have seen, makes similar claims "of olde under the Law of Nature."[71] The mutual obligations within this theory assign to the father love and nuture of the children and to the children obedience and reverence for the father. Because he is writing to shore up both paternal and regal authority at the same time, Bodin stresses both the natural and biblical authority for children's obedience and care:

> And as the Father is by nature bound to nourish his children according to his abilitie, and to instruct them in all civilitie and vertue: so the children also when they are once grown up are bound, but with a much more straiter bond, to love, reverence, serve, and nourish their Father, and in all things to shew themselves dutifull and obedient unto them, and by all meanes to hide and cover their infirmities and imperfections, if they see any in them, and never to spare their lives and goods to save the life of them by whom they themselves tooke breath.[72]

This understanding of patriarchal thought can provide answers to Bevington's question about Shakespeare's reversion to older models of the romance, for the genre provides not only providential natural settings in which to mythologize power structures, but also allows the dramatist to portray the ruler as father, pure and simple. Thus Shakespeare avoids one of the deep contradictions that invades patriarchal thought at the moment when the father "steps from the house into the street. For if kings are fathers, fathers cannot be patriarchs. If fathers are patriarchs at home, kings cannot be patriarchs on their thrones. Patriarchal kings and patriarchal fathers are a contradiction in terms."[73] Bodin, as we have seen, solved this problem by claiming the father-children relationship as a model for kingship, but he did not claim that the ruler-subject relationship was natural. The genre of romance provides Shakespeare another solution: the ruler can be shown almost entirely in his familial relationships, and so the power represented is simple and natural. With rare exceptions the actions of the romances center in families, which according to patriarchal definitions would include servants as well as blood relations. The conflicts in the plays lie within families, and the romances deal centrally with the anxieties of fatherhood for the ruler. The death of a child is a threat to father and state in every action, and the ultimate recovery of progeny for the succession forms its happy conclusion. The ruler's tyranny—or abuse of power by others—frequently takes the form of harming children. Fatherhood presents other anxieties: one's progeny may be illegitimate; incest may be a temptation; children can rebel and fail to marry in the interests of the state, or, if they are sons, anticipate too eagerly one's mortality. All these conflicts are apparently resolved—evaded really—in the self-correcting structures of romance.

Although Cymbeline pays tribute to Rome, the rulers of the romances seem to possess absolute power, largely because we see them dealing almost exclusively with their families and retainers. And Pericles, Cymbeline, Leontes, and Prospero are all given to tyranny (Pericles only momentarily) and find their ways back from it through their families. Shakespeare seems to have understood the narcissistic rage that can overcome the father as a real threat to his rule, for his portraits of it from Lear through Leontes to Prospero are searing. Each ruler reforms, not through a greater sense of justice, a theme hardly known in these plays, but through feminization, through the recovery or development of his "woman's part." This is signalled by the recovery of a daughter or a wife or by the forgiveness of old enemies or some combination of these.

Although all the romances center in families, *The Winter's Tale* is the most interesting study of the anxieties of fatherhood. Marital jealousy is rapidly transformed into questions of the legitimacy and control of offspring. With Hermione pregnant as the play opens and Polixenes a visitor of nine months, Leontes's jealousy instantly becomes the questioning of the fatherhood of the expected child, and then the suspicion is hysterically extended to Mamillius as well. Mamillius's importance to the realm is established early. Archidamus tells Camillo, "You have an unspeakable comfort of your young prince Mamillius: it is a gentleman of the greatest promise that ever came into my note" (1.1.39ff.). Polixenes longs to see his son again and so will return to Bohemia; he and Leontes compete, as in all things, in doting on their sons. Polixenes says that Florizel "with his varying childness cures in me / Thoughts that would thick my blood" (1.2.170–71), but Leontes's joy in Mamillius is quickly blighted by his jealousy. His imagination dwells on Mamillius's resemblance to him: "They say we are / Almost as like as eggs" (1.2.129–30), and later he notes Florizel's resemblance to Polixenes (5.1.124–26).[74] But as his madness grows, Leontes isolates himself from his grieving son for fear of weakening his purposed revenge. Throughout the first two acts there is continued emphasis on the damage Leontes's jealousy does to Mamillius. The climax of this theme is Leontes's order for the murder of Perdita, which is only softened to desertion of the child in a remote place. The nightmare of the patriarchy's dependence on great creating female nature is that the unchaste wife will bear false generations because we live on a bawdy planet.

Yet the trials of paternity do not cease with the birth of legitimate issue. A further problem is the obedience of adult children. They can be a special burden to the father who is a king because on the child's marriage depends the future of the realm. Thus the second part of *The Winter's Tale* is dominated by Polixenes as the parallel winter figure, spying on Florizel in anxious concern over his heir's love for a seeming shepherdess. Polixenes is a descendent of the spying disguised rulers of Chapter Two. He is deeply shaken by his son's behavior, both because Florizel casually anticipates his father's death (an oedipal wish for power without rivalry for the mother's love) and because he refuses to consider revealing his match with Perdita to his father. Polixenes repeats the experience of Leontes: he almost loses the heir to his kingdom as a result of his tyrannical rage. Florizel will be true to his vow to Perdita, which he identifies with the fecundity of nature:

> It cannot fail but by
> The violation of my faith; and then
> Let nature crush the sides o' th' earth together
> And mar the seeds within! Lift up thy looks:
> From my succession wipe me, father; I
> Am heir to my affection.
> (4.4.485–90)

Meanwhile in Sicily courtiers are urging Leontes to marry to insure the succession, but the oracle has said that Leontes will not have an heir until his lost child is found. When she is found, Leontes experiences the full scope of his loss through looking at Florizel and Perdita: "What might I have been, / Might I a son and daughter now have look'd on, / Such goodly things as you!" (5.1.176–78). The possible loss of succession in two kingdoms is averted by Leontes's recovery of Perdita and the verification of her identity, but the play acknowledges costs in the death of Mamillius, even though he is "replaced" by Florizel.

The anxieties about paternity experienced by Leontes and Polixenes cause the play's conflicts: the patriarch's dependence on women and children lies at the heart of both men's torment. Is this child mine? Will this child obey me? "Kings are no less unhappy, their issue not being gracious, than they are in losing them when they have approved their virtues" (4.1.29–32). Against the male rage at this predicament, Shakespeare sets up a female network (including Camillo and the shepherd) which averts the potential tragedy.[75] The splitting of the female figure into Hermoine, Paulina, and Perdita allows Shakespeare to present complex dimensions of female values. In each character a set of aspects may be dominant, without stinting the varied facets of personality that keep her from hardening into a symbol. Hermione develops from associations with fertility, sexuality, wit, and charm to the quintessential good wife when under attack, and then, after a nun-like existence for sixteen years, to a figure of grace and forgiveness. Paulina is allowed a great deal of power, even in the court, but it is used for nurturing and her devotion to others, as she and her arts become Leontes's path back to Perdita and Hermione. Perdita is associated with nature, with fertility that repeats her mother's at the beginning, and with a youthful sexuality that is still respectful of social forms. Taken together, they assure the play's outcome, yet we should not overlook the troublesome sixteen-year gap in the action. While the interval allows Perdita to mature, Hermione is passing her childbearing years, and the play exchanges the witty, assertive mother, a potential equal of Leontes, for the lively but more sedate daughter, over whom the father has natural authority. However triumphant the women might seem at the end of *The Winter's Tale*, the forgiveness of Leontes by Hermione once again signals, as in the comedies, the acceptance by women of an asymmetrical relationship in the greater male privilege to err with impunity.[76] Thus, with much relief, Leontes immediately begins to give orders after his reconciliation with Hermione, and although his first order is to find Paulina a suitable husband in the nurturing Camillo, his behavior makes clear that the power and resources of women are once again used to sustain the patriarchy. The ruler has needed to absorb female values which preserve life, but those values do not alter his power. He still possesses total authority, which absorbs and controls female creativity.

Leontes's recovery of his family and his faith in nature is a complex version of the simple paradigm in *Pericles,* where the recovery of Marina heals Pericles's despair, the vision of Diana leads his thoughts from revenge on Cleon to a reunion with Thaisa (5.2.253–56), and Marina is quickly wedded by Pericles to the ruler Lysimachus, who has already been attracted to her by her natural nobility. The father's relationship to his daughter gives meaning to his life and a future to his dynasty through her marriage to a politically acceptable object. Here, too, the wife of the ruler is absent during her fertile years and is replaced by a nubile daughter, whose procreativity is put in the service of the patriarchy.[77] With his absolute power, Pericles is prevented from tyranny by assimilating what Posthumus calls the woman's part. Pericles is drawn from revenge to Thaisa by a vision of Diana, just as Leontes is led back to trust in female values by Paulina. Cymbeline and Prospero express this assimilation by the forgiveness of old enemies, a gesture usually reserved, as in *The Winter's Tale,* for women.

In a variance of the pattern, Cymbeline recovers his sons and Imogen loses a kingdom thereby. The conflicts within society arise because of dislocations within families. The Queen alienates Cymbeline from Imogen and plans to poison her after the match with Cloten fails. Belarius has robbed Cymbeline of his sons because of an earlier betrayal, "thinking to bar thee of succession" (3.3.102). These concerns cause Cymbeline and Posthumus to wrong Imogen because she is the only heir to the throne. Her father would have her marry Cloten, even though Posthumus's merit is obvious to all and he has been raised as part of the royal family. The question of Posthumus's true value as a person is raised when he marries Imogen, and henceforth he is valued in Britain and abroad according to Imogen's rank as a princess, "rather by her value than his own" (1.4.14). This predicament forms the basis for Posthumus's jealousy and the nearly fatal wager.

So before Posthumus is reconciled with Imogen, Shakespeare gives him a vision of his own family,[78] which is a close parallel to Imogen's: he also had two brothers who fought the Romans valiantly for Britain. Thus Shakespeare provides the "more equal ballasting" Imogen longs for when she meets her brothers (3.6.76–79). Imogen happily loses the kingdom and Posthumus has better sources of esteem than those he began with. Imogen's attitudes should not escape our notice. The power of women in these plays is strictly procreative and conciliatory: even the spunkiest of them has no desire for political authority, especially if it disturbs her husband's equilibrium.

Cymbeline has been wrongheaded for longer than his marriage to the Queen as we see in his treatment of Belarius, and so he must not only lose the influence of his step-family but regain his natural family before he can integrate the woman's part into his character, as his use of childbirth images suggests (5.5.368–70). After being reunited with his children Cymbeline pardons Belarius, Lucius, and finally Posthumus, who quickly forgives Iachimo, though with a toughness that lends a distinctly masculine tone to the gesture: "The pow'r that I have on you is to spare you; / The malice toward you to forgive you. Live, / And deal with others better" (5.5.418–20). It has been the "woman's part" to forgive, just as Imogen forgives both Iachimo and Posthumus: so the forgiveness by Posthumus and Cymbeline signals their acceptance of female values, which are identified with nature and Cymbeline's natural family. Posthumus's famous image of reunion with Imogen underscores this association: "Hang there like fruit, my soul, / Till the tree die" (5.5.263–64). Moreover, reconciliation with Imogen seems necessary for males to reach significant female elements within themselves and to be generous and giving: she is a catalyst to the process.

Although the other romances show fathers reunited with their families, *The Tempest* takes its fathers through the experience of loss in a play which seems virtually to equate children and political power. To teach Alonso his crime in helping Antonio usurp Milan, Prospero lets Alonso believe he has lost his son. The dependence of both aging rulers on their children is made emphatic in *The Tempest* through Alonso's supposed loss of Ferdinand and through Prospero's having raised Miranda. Alonso begins to regret past actions as he mourns "mine heir / Of Naples and of Milan," acknowledging that although he may own the cause of the disaster, so he owns "the dear'st of the loss" (2.1.140). Ferdinand's "death" and Claribel's remoteness give encouragement to Sebastian in plotting to take Alonso's crown. When Alonso sees the vision of the banquet, he decides to partake, even if the meal is his last, "since I feel / The best is past" (3.3.50–51). In the same scene Ariel tells Alonso that "the powers" have bereft him of his son because of his crimes, and this throws Alonso into suicidal despair. He is still frantic when the court party is brought to confront Prospero and tells him of Ferdinand, "Irreparable is the loss, and patience / Says it is past her cure" (5.1.140–41). When Prospero is certain of Alonso's repentance, Prospero tells him of his similar grief and then reveals Ferdinand and Miranda playing chess. All of Alonso's experience on the island is invested in Ferdinand, and Prospero uses it to bring him to the very heart of loss and back.

Similarly Prospero assures Miranda at the beginning of the play, "I have done nothing but in care of thee, / Of thee my dear one, thee my daughter" (1.1.16–17). Prospero is the single father in the romances who, instead of losing and regaining his daughter, raises her to the time when he must lose her to marriage. This situation gives him maximum control of her life—when crossed he calls her his foot—but it also centers his life in her: "O, a cherubin / Thou wast that did preserve me!" (1.2.152–53). So Prospero carefully engineers the romance of Ferdinand and Miranda, quickly has Ferdinand in his complete control, and is constantly presiding over the brief courtship of the couple. Yet, when Ferdinand has undergone the tests, when Miranda has been taught about the new world she will enter, and they have pledged themselves to one another, Prospero begins to relinquish his control of them, and as he gives Miranda to Ferdinand, the intensity of Prospero's feeling for her is palpable:

> If I have too austerely punished you,
> Your compensation makes amends; for I
> Have given you here a third of mine own life,
> Or that for which I live; who once again
> I tender to thy hand. All thy vexations
> Were but trials of thy love, and thou
> Hast strangely stood the test. Here, afore heaven,
> I ratify this my rich gift. O Ferdinand,
> Do not smile at me that I boast her off,
> For thou shalt find she will outstrip all praise
> And make it halt behind her.
>
> (4.1.1–11)

Although Prospero's praise of Miranda makes her seem highly valued, it should not blind us to the fact that Miranda remains an object of exchange between Prospero and Ferdinand. Her basic relationship to men is to wonder at them, a reciprocation of the meaning of her name: "to be wondered at." Prospero's love for her masks the dependence his domination of her implies, a dependence she never challenges and which he must outgrow.

The maturing of the young people means loss to their parents but brings prospect of issue, which will be a consolation for the mortality of the fathers, a theme which becomes important toward the end of the play. The linkage is clear at the end of the wedding masque, which has been so emphatic about progeny, when Prospero explains to Ferdinand the source of his distemper:

> We are such stuff
> As dreams are made on, and our little life
> Is rounded with a sleep. Sir, I am vexed.
> Bear with my weakness; my old brain is troubled.
> Be not disturbed with my infirmity.
>
> (4.1.156–60)

Prospero, the true patriarch, explains all significant information to Ferdinand, not to the dear daughter. As he prepares to relinquish his absolute control of the island and its creatures (freeing Ariel and Caliban) for the risks of reigning in Milan again, Prospero also faces his own mortality: "Every third thought shall be my grave" (5.1.312). The phrase echoes his earlier description of Miranda, who is "a third of mine own life."

The process by which Prospero overcomes his impulse to revenge differs from those of the other rulers, all of whom experience the recovery of a daughter and have the benign influence of a woman—or the loss of an evil one—to guide them away from tyranny. For Prospero to accept influence from one he denotes his "foot" would strain credibility, and so Shakespeare uses the Neoplatonic hierarchy to good purpose in having Ariel, the spirit, teach humanity to his learned, angry master. As a superhuman spirit temporarily controlled by magic, Ariel seems the only member of Prospero's strange little family from whom the magus could learn. Prospero differs from the other rulers in being quite distant from women, as Kahn points out.[79] Kermode explains this celibacy as a necessity of his art,[80] and we should add that as women have no place in the austere life of a magus, so they are not attached to the process by which Prospero relinquishes the magic of the island, with its illusions of omnipotence: women have as little to do with power as possible. All these rulers must rise above the impulse to revenge, which ties one inevitably to the past, as Shakespeare understood. Instead of repeating the past, the romances present it as prologue to a hopeful future in the younger generation, whose succession to the power of the fathers is the life stream of the patriarchy.

Succession

Even if the identity of Elizabeth's successor had not been a matter of long-term anxiety, especially in her later years, the succession would be a predictable feature of these patriarchal romances. Some reasons are historical. The debates and anxiety about the succession to the English throne did not disappear after James had been welcomed to rule the English. His claim was defended from Jesuit arguments against it through assertions that primogenitive succession was ordained by God: "the succession of children, is one of the primary precepts of nature."[81] James was, of course, descended from Henry VII, and the doctrine of the king's two bodies could explain his being Elizabeth's heir to meet arguments,[82] such as those of Hooker, that the hereditary monarchy reverted to the people if there was a failure of heirs.[83] But there remained the problem that James had been born a Scot, and that fact kept the question of the succession before the Commons for the first five years of James's reign because of his continuing requests for the union of Scotland and England. Furthermore, his having a family was one indisputable advantage he could claim over his awesome predecessor. In his first address to Parliament James was careful to remind his new subjects that he enjoyed a succession from his body which assured continuity in the realm: "Now although these blessings before rehearsed of Inward and Outward peace, be great: yet seeing that in all things, a great part of their goodnesse and estimation is lost, if they haue not appearance of perpetuity or long continuance; so hath it pleased Almighty God to accompany my person also with that favour, hauing healthful and hopefull Issue of my body, whereof some are here present, for continuance and propogation of that vndoubted right which is in my Person."[84] *The Basilicon Doron* was, of course, written for Prince Henry, whom James called "my naturall and lawfull successor . . . the first fruits of Gods blessing towards me in my posteritie."[85] The ostensible purpose of the book was to guide James's successor in preparing to assume the throne. A step along that way was Henry's investiture as Prince of Wales in 1610, an occasion for which Ben Jonson wrote *Prince Henry's Barriers.* This masque ends with a prophecy of Merlin in which the splendid future of the royal family is envisioned:

> You, and your other you, great king and queen,
> Have yet the least of your bright fortune seen,
> Which shall rise brighter every hour with time,
> And in your pleasure quite forget the crime
> Of change; your age's night shall be her noon.[86]

Merlin foresees achievements of state for Henry, conquests in war for Charles, and as for Elizabeth, "she shall be / Mother of nations, and her princes see / Rivals almost to these" (421–23). For James genealogy was destiny. His contribution to political theory "lay in identifying his prerogative with the production of a legitimate male successor. Unlike his Tudor predecessor, James located his power in a royal line that proceeded from him; for him, as for many European absolutists, legitimacy was asserted in genealogy. The kingdom was, quite literally, in his body, the arcana made flesh."[87]

The romances assume, then, that kingly reproduction naturally reproduces the state. But if Shakespeare's plays were conforming narrowly to the Stuart ideology, the successors would be male. In the plays where he is tied to history, *Henry VIII* or *Cymbeline,* Shakespeare is frank about the ruler's need for male heirs. Why, then, does Shakespeare choose to make the succession move through daughters when he has artistic freedom from history, especially in view of James's published theories? Critics have speculated about the question and have presented a variety of possible answers, such a variety that Shakespeare's decision seems overdetermined. Some arguments are historical: the so-called Elizabethan revival and the inheritance patterns among noble families of the early Stuart era.

The concept of an Elizabethan revival in Jacobean times is based on a growing adulation of Elizabeth I, as James's popularity waned.[88] As Frances Yates describes it, this movement consisted of a self-conscious evocation of Elizabethan chivalric imperialism as a heritage for the Stuarts, especially for Prince Henry, and a strong identification of Princess Elizabeth with her Tudor namesake. Yates claims that *Prince Henry's Barriers* shows the prince as a chivalric hero in a work that echoes Elizabeth's Accession Day Tilts: "It is a symbolism which gives prominence to the older generation—James must always receive chief honour as the monarch—but the second generation, the generation of his children, stand forth as the inheritors of the promise."[89] Crucial in this argument is Prince Henry's death, for, according to Yates, after that loss, Elizabeth, who was married to the head of the Union of German Protestant Princes, became the focus of imagination for those who wanted to restore a more aggressive protestant policy than James favored. Although the adulation of Elizabeth is palpable at the end of *Henry VIII*, the general argument about the Elizabethan revival as a reading of the last plays makes them captive of a single political viewpoint, one too narrow for richly multivalent work. Yet, if we cannot accept the general interpretation of the plays, the Elizabethan revival may have been a factor in Shakespeare's choice of daughters for the succession.

Furthermore, we should recognize that these obedient daughters who marry suitable mates and serve the patriarchy with their generativity provide a heartening fantasy for the male society in dealing with one sort of power—a disruptive one—which women actually possessed in Shakespeare's England: inheritance by lineal descent. A society based on primogeniture can be preoccupied with running out of males in any propertied family. As Lisa Jardine points out, there was an effort at the time to keep lands within immediate families which lacked male heirs by leaving them to the eldest daughter:

> In the sixteenth century, entailed land (land for which a strict sequence of inheritance was legally specified) either passed in *tail male* (from eldest son to eldest son) or in *tail general* (to the eldest child of either sex). Increasingly in the latter half of the sixteenth century and the early part of the seventeenth, families made efforts to convert *tail male* into *tail general* to avoid

alienation of lands outside the immediate family to distant male relatives. A number of factors contributed to this change of strategy away from strict male succession to one involving daughters as direct heirs; the most obvious was the dearth of male heirs amongst the nobility.[90]

Jardine argues, and I think rightly, that anxiety about decisions women might make as carriers of wealth[91] makes strong women threatening to a Jacobean audience, and that if they make independent choices, as does the Duchess of Malfi, they are destroyed. (It should be noted, however, that the Duchess's son inherits his mother's rights.) Shakespeare's docile Marina or Miranda, through whom a succession to rule could pass undisturbed, represent a reassuring patriarchal ideal, which raises and then allays the anxiety about women who inherit power.

Psychological critics have submitted another set of explanations for Shakespeare's choice of daughters as successors. Cyrus Hoy has stressed the asexuality of the relationships between father and daughter, as contrasted, of course, with the husband-wife relationship; Barber has discussed the liberation of the family "from the threat of sexual degradation"; and Kahn has argued that the daughter gives a man his patriarchal identity without the oedipal conflicts a son presents.[92] Surely the casualness with which Florizel anticipates his father's death and even Ferdinand his succession shows Shakespeare's awareness of oedipal conflicts. On another tack, Erickson stresses the effects of the social hierarchy in constraining female generativity.[93]

From the ideological perspective of naturalizing political structures advanced in this chapter, the daughter's succession makes a process seem natural which would be more clearly political if the son succeeded: the strategy disguises the political in simple human terms. The succession is no less important to Leontes than to Cymbeline; yet one has a much stronger sense of the institutional nature of the succession where Imogen's brothers replace her than where the daughter gives life to her father and the state. The rhetoric of political theory supports this argument, for it too translates political relationships into terms of love and caring—traditional female values, in short. We can recall here Bodin's words about the obligation of adult children to "love, reverence, serve, and nourish their Father."[94] In the same chapter Bodin gives revealing historical examples. Those dealing with sons concentrate on the great severity with which Roman fathers treated them. The extended example concerning a daughter describes a woman who secretly "gave sucke unto her father condemned to be pined [starved] to death."[95] After the jailer told the magistrates about this act of piety, the father was pardoned and a temple built in honor of the daughter. Other versions of the story appear in books about women during the sixteenth and seventeenth centuries. In C. N. Agrippa's *Of the Nobilitie and Excellencie of Womankynde* (1542) a young woman who nurses her mother in prison is an example of pity and saves her mother's life: "And of that prison, they made a Temple, and called it, the temple of Pitie."[96] A version of this ancient story appears in Christine de Pizan's *The Book of the City of Ladies;* in Pizan's story the jailed parent is also a mother. Later versions of the same story occur in *An Apologie for Woman-kinde* (1605) and Thomas Heywood's *Gynaikeion* (1624).[97] In *An Apologie* two examples are given, one saving a father and one a mother, while in Heywood a mother is rescued. The first thought this story evokes for the Shakespearean is Lear's "kind nursery." But Pericles, Cymbeline, Leontes, and Prospero do not anticipate being cared for by their daughters, who are nonetheless perceived as life-giving. The image conveyed in Bodin's legend is a central one for women in authoritarian society: the mother without sexuality. The daughter who gives life to her parent is mothering without the threat that sexuality might present to the social order.[98] Motherhood is essential to succession, which ultimately depends upon female generativity. Yet the patriarchy, as we have said, controls reproduction: "the facts of life serve the powers of the state."[99] Dependent as it may be upon motherhood, an authoritarian regime is always suspicious of the disruptive element in sexuality: hence, the constant threat of sexual degradation Barber notes in the romances. The daughter in the exempla of Bodin, Agrippa, and Heywood, like the daughters in *Pericles, Cymbeline,* and *The Winter's Tale,* gives life without sex when reunited with the parent, but still as daughter, not wife. Thus Perdita gives life to both Leontes and Hermione, who has survived to see her daughter. Prospero is similarly kept alive by Miranda. The story worships the generativity and nurturing of women in the temple dedicated to pity, while keeping womankind subservient to the parental order.

By keeping the wife invisible during her childbearing years and focussing on the daughter, the plays accent the chastity which patriarchal societies emphasize to control female sexuality. Bacon's *New Atlantis* is quite open about the importance of chastity in its ideal society:

> You shall understand that there is not under the heavens so chaste a nation as this of Bensalem, nor so free from all pollution or foulness. . . . For there is nothing amongst mortal men more fair and admirable than the chaste minds of this people. Know therefore that with them there are no stews, no dissolute houses, no courtesans, nor any thing of that kind. Nay they wonder (with detestation) at you in Europe, which permit such things. They say ye have put marriage out of office, for marriage is ordained a remedy for unlawful concupiscence, and natural concupiscence seemeth as a spur to marriage.[100]

Certainly Marina, reformer of a brothel, Perdita, Miranda, and the slightly chilly Imogen would all be comfortable in such a setting. Although the daughters are safely chaste, there is the threat of sexual abuse in each play: incest, prostitution, intended rapists or seducers, the thought of infidelity. In *The Tempest,* for example, rampant sexuality in Caliban and Prospero's suspicion of it in Ferdinand justify stringent social control of man and monster, who are linked through a series of parallels. By making the daughters as chaste as Bensalem, but surrounding them with the excesses of Europe, Shakespeare combines the reassuring demeanor of the young people with "freeing family ties from the threat of sexual degradation."[101]

Myths about the natural processes of birth and mothering and their appropriation by the political structures are accomplished by a series of transformations: a fusing of the generations so that the child mothers the parent and the doctrine of the king's two bodies, under which the sexes may change and either sex may reproduce asexually.

Much rhetoric about the royal succession depended, especially in the reign of Elizabeth, upon the legal and mythical doctrine of the king's two bodies, one of which is natural, and one, political or corporate. The first body may be a minor, senile, sick, and may die; the other is ageless, immortal, and sexless, like the angels. Under this doctrine's aegis, a female, Elizabeth, is called a king or a prince. Edward Forset explains the concept: "the king in his personall respects . . . is as one man, single and indiuiduall, yet as in the right of Soveraigntie, he gayneth the appellation and capacities of a corporation . . . the resplendence and power of soveraigntie in the royall person of a Soveraigne, shewing itselfe both in so great maiestie, as dazeleth the eyes of all beholders, and in so admirable effects, as to transforme sauagenesse into ciuilitie, repugnances into concords, vices into vertues."[102] The most frequent metaphor used to convey the succession according to this doctrine was the phoenix, which was especially apt because it was asexual and "because it reproduced no more than one individuation at a time, the incumbent."[103] This is, of course, precisely the image Shakespeare used for the succession from Elizabeth to James at the end of *Henry VIII*:

> Nor shall this peace sleep with her; but as when
> The bird of wonder dies, the maiden phoenix,
> Her ashes new create another heir,
> As great in admiration as herself,
> So shall she leave her blessedness to one,
> When heaven shall call her from this cloud of darkness,
> Who from the sacred ashes of her honor
> Shall star-like rise, as great in fame as she was,
> And so stand fix'd.
>
> (5.5.40–48)

This process of asexual reproduction of heirs to the kingdom may explain the appropriation by Pericles and Cymbeline of the language of procreation, as well as their tendency to describe the regaining of their successors as miraculous. When Pericles begins to suspect that the young woman trying to heal his despair is his lost daughter, he uses birth imagery: "I am great with woe, and shall deliver weeping" (5.1.106). When he is sure of Marina's identity, he uses an image of a miraculous conception: "Thou that beget'st him that did thee beget" (5.1.200). And, as Cymbeline recovers not only Imogen but also his long-lost sons, he exclaims, "O, what am I / A mother to the birth of three? Ne'er mother / Rejoic'd deliverance more" (5.5.370–72). The temporary loss of the ruler's children strongly emphasizes, as in *The Tempest,* the need for the succession, and the reunion with the father (without the mother) makes possible the illusion of the miraculous, phoenix-like birth of the successor. We can now understand the importance of the separations and reunions in the romances, for they not only allow the miraculous substitution of Florizel for Mamillius, but also the illusion of the father giving birth: "Patriarchalism is a regular feature of family life in which the natural event of procreation becomes the extension of male prerogative and male power."[104] The scattering of the family conveys the dire need of the parent for children, as shown by the despair it brings to Alonso or Pericles. Then the reunion of father with child, which always takes place before that with their mother, allows for the illusion of their birth to the father alone. The parent-child relationship is entirely reciprocal: each appears to have given life to the other asexually.

Even in humble surroundings, these heirs have been carefully brought up, usually by men, for "the Father of his fatherly duty is bound to care for the nourishing, education, and vertuous government of his children."[105] Belarius, a double for Cymbeline, has taught Guiderius and Aviragus of courts, of princes, of the tricks of war, subjects to fashion nobility, for he knows they are royal, and, as we have seen, he teaches them respect even for Cloten's rank. Although they are valiant in war, they are also courteous. Perdita, too, is raised in a foster home, but she has been taught respect for rank that exceeds Florizel's. She is a gracious hostess at the festival, encouraged by the shepherd on the model of his late wife. Marina knows that she is royal, and she is so accomplished that she overshadows Philoten and earns Dionyza's envy. Like Cymbeline's sons, she is respectful of the dead: she is strewing Lychorida's grave with flowers when first we see her. Her accomplishments are the traditional ones for a woman, but they earn her release from the brothel. Miranda's education is the finest of all, as her father has planned her destiny and tutored her himself:

> here
> Have I, thy schoolmaster, made thee more profit
> Than other princess' can that have more time
> For vainer hours and tutors not so careful.
>   (1.2.171–74)

They are a decorous lot, who could have grown up in Bacon's Bensalem. The self-correcting structures of the romance soften even modest revolt, for although Imogen and Florizel marry against their fathers' wills, their rebellions need not be forgiven because the plots avoid the consequences. Imogen loses the kingdom, and Florizel has married a princess. The women are not colorless: Marina and Perdita are self-sufficient, and Imogen has real spirit. Only Miranda seems pale, but even she woos for herself (3.1.67–91). Yet, taken together, both men and women seem tame fowl after the energetic couples of the romantic comedies.

These gentle young people may be a glimpse of what Mervyn James calls "the civil society" in his study of the Durham region. After the Northern Rising, he says, the lineage society, in which a few great families dominated the region with ostentatious households and mighty followings, gave way, as "literacy and education spread among the upper classes, to an insistence on magnanimity and a cultivated taste as the marks of true gentility. As a result, the essence of nobility came to be seen as the marriage of ancient lineage and decorous deportment."[106] In this sense, the romances move beyond *Lear,* resembling the spirit of Book VI of *The Fairie Queene:*

These three on men all gracious gifts bestow,
Which decke the body and adorne the mynde,
To make them lovely or well fauoured show,
As comely carriage, entertainment kynde,
Sweete semblaunt, friendly offices that bynde,
And all the complements of curtesie:
They teach us, how to each degree and kynde
We should our selves demeane, to low, to hie;
To friends, to foes, which skill men call Civility.[107]

Even in youth, the new generation seem protopatriarchs. In killing for the kingship, Macbeth knows what he has sacrificed: "that which should accompany old age, / As honor, love, obedience, troops of friends, / I must not look to have" (5.3.24–26). But the sweet-natured Ferdinand seems already old as he assures Prospero that he will behave toward Miranda so as to enjoy all that Macbeth has cast away:

As I hope
For quiet days, fair issue, and long life,
With such love as 'tis now, the murkiest den,
The most opportune place, the strongest suggestion
Our worser genius can, shall never melt
Mine honor into lust, to take away
The edge of that day's celebration
When I shall think or Phoebus' steeds are founder'd
Or Night kept chain'd below.

(4.1.23–31)

Islands and Power

James had little compunction about claiming absolute and inalienable power for the king. As he had more trouble with Commons, he insisted more on the theme. In 1609 he declared to Parliament: "The State of *Monarchie* is the supremest thing vpon earth: For kings are not only *Gods* Lieutenants vpon earth, and sit vpon *Gods* throne, but euen by *God* himselfe they are called Gods."[108] The power of life and death Bodin attributed to the father over his children, James

attributed to the king in relation to his subjects. Others, like
Forset, made similar arguments: that Parliament, courts, and
all officers were under the sovereign, whose will was law.
While such ideas were circulated in political pamphlets, the
court masques, especially those of Jonson, present an ideology where gradually James is not only called the greatest
monarch in the world, but is regarded as one who can control nature as well as society.

If father-rulers had not just the power of life and death
over their subject-children, which Bodin and James claimed
for them, but something more—the power to give life—they
could pretend through artistic illusion, not just that their
power was natural, but that it was supernatural, that it could
control nature. Recent work by Stephen Orgel and Jonathan
Goldberg has made us aware of the extent to which Jonson's
masques assign godly power to James: "Annually he transforms winter into spring, renders the savage wilderness benign, makes the earth fruitful, restores the Golden Age."[109]
Although Jonson's masques may not be as monologic as this
description implies,[110] they frequently represent a king who
not only rules according to nature, but also rules nature, as
here in *Oberon* (1611):

> 'Tis he that stays the time from turning old,
> And keeps the age up in a head of gold;
> That in his own true circle still doth run,
> And holds his course as certain as the sun.
> He makes it ever day and ever spring
> Where he doth shine, and quickens everything
> Like a new nature; so that true to call
> Him by his title is to say, he's all.[111]

Prospero's magic can seem a version of Jonson's representations of Stuart power, as Orgel believes, and as Frank Kermode suggested years ago:

> It has been objected that Shakespeare could not have present-
> ed at the Court of James I a play openly alluding to a system
> of magic to which the King was notoriously opposed. But

> James was well accustomed to such treatment; he himself was often presented as a beneficent magician, and he took pleasure in Jonson's *Masque of Queens,* a brilliant iceberg whose hidden part is a craggy mass of occult learning. He no more took exception to this than he did to the presentation of pagan gods whom he theoretically regarded as devils, because he understood the equation between a fiction of beneficent magic and the sacred power he himself possessed as an actual king.[112]

Yet Orgel and Kermode have made a closer identity of Prospero and James than the play will bear, for where the masques remain transparent in not exposing the art of their illusions and stay mythical in Barthes's sense, *The Tempest* exposes the limitations of Prospero's magic, shows the island as untransformed, and gives power to the audience at the end. The play invites the audience to understand how the patriarchal ideology uses nature: "It is the gap between nature and power that political rhetoric transforms. It is the space in which patriarchal rhetoric is constructed, the space of the mystification of power."[113]

The masques frequently mystify the unity of the island of Great Britain, which James urged upon Parliament and which was always represented in Stuart propaganda as a greater triumph than the union of the roses by Henry VII.[114] So whenever James's descent from Henry was mentioned, it was accompanied by the unification of the kingdoms. Here is the new king in 1603: "First, by my descent lineally out of the loynes of *Henry* the seventh, is reunited and confirmed in mee the Union of the two Princely Roses of the two Houses of LANCASTER and YORKE, whereof that King of happy memorie was the first Vniter . . . But the Vnion of these princely Houses, is nothing comparable to the Vnion of two ancient and famous Kingdomes, which is the other inward Peace annexed to my Person."[115] His formulation was echoed by Thomas Adams in a sermon, "The Citie of Peace": "*Henricas Rosas, Regna Jacobus:* in Henry was the union of the Roses, in James of the Kingdomes."[116] James saw himself fulfilling a divinely ordained, natural destiny:

> Hath not God first vnited these two Kingdomes both in Language, Religion, and similitude of maners? Yea, hath hee not made us all in one Island, compassed with one Sea, and of it selfe by nature so indiuisible, as almost those that were borderers themselves . . . cannot distinguish . . . their own limits? . . . And now in the end and fullnesse of time vnited, the right and title of both in my Person, . . . whereby it is now become a little World within it selfe, being intrenched and fortified round about with a naturall, and yet admirable strong pond or ditch, whereby all the former feares of this Nation are now quite cut off.[117]

Jonson's wedding masque *Hymenaei* (1606) made the union of the wedding into the unity of the kingdoms: "*Hymenaei* is not only a formal wedding masque; *Hymenaei* is a dramatic and symbolic representation of the Union of the kingdoms as it was conceived in the propaganda issued by men who had approval of the king himself."[118] During *Prince Henry's Barriers* (1611) Merlin reviews the achievements of the English kings in trade and industry, in war and conquest, alluding again to Henry VII and his descendant:

> Henry but joined the roses that ensigned
> Particular families, but this hath joined
> The rose and thistle, and in them combined
> A union that shall never be declined.[119]

The Stuart ideology continued an identification of the king's absolute rule with the unity of the island, so that by the end of James's reign, all the elements of the myth were firmly in place. The last chapter of Francis Markham's *The Book of Honour* (1625) was devoted to the absolute king, one who is responsible only to God and whose kingdom he can control entirely. Markham did a survey of the kingdoms of Europe and discovered that France had conflicts with the Pope, while Spain not only shared those conflicts, but also had lands that were too vast to control. To no one's great surprise, only James of Britain was the perfect absolute ruler because his realm was a united island, large enough to be powerful and small enough to govern conveniently:

And this was one sacred and puissant King James, of this Ile, Monarch of *Great Britaine and Ireland;* he that from the very Conquest of this Ile, was able (notwithstanding all the turmoiles and contrarities of State) to derive himselfe the undoubted, true, and onely absolute Heire to all his Dominions; hee that by a blessed descent, and a blessed coniunction, first brought the Monarchy of this Iland together, and buckled them so fast, as they are never to be divided; he that had no more than he can well gripe, and yet so much, and with so fast a hold, as was able to make his proudest enemies to tremble, whose kingdomes are so allied, and naturally depend on one another, that nowe that he hath taken downe the partition wall from betweene them, they are incorporate, and can no more be sundred, but by infinite loss and desolation.[120]

In *Cymbeline* Shakespeare made a Virgilian association of Britain, the swan's nest, as a separate and favored place (Et penitus toto divisos orbe).[121] It is a fortunate isle. The notion was a popular one;[122] Jonson referred to it continually in his masques.[123] The idea is related to the ancient notion of Britain as one of the Fortunate Isles because its mild climate seemed to the Romans miraculous. It was frequently compared to Sicily, linked with the Hesperides and with the Islands of the Blest. Iachimo feels the effect of the air in Britain, and its climate is transforming for Posthumus. The island is a world apart, and its nature is beneficent to human beings. The play also evokes the Tudor myths in Wales and Britain's ancient past, which the Stuarts liked to connect to their own myths.

But *The Tempest* works in another way. Prospero's island, in contrast, is not idealized. As we have said, it is a barren place owned by Sycorax and Caliban and taken by Prospero as a colonist. The island is one over which Prospero enjoys absolute control, to be sure, for Caliban, Ariel, and Prospero have complete knowledge of it. Yet it is assuredly not one of the Fortunate Isles: it is a place of refuge for Prospero and Miranda until their enemies are brought within the range of Prospero's magic. It is neither a utopia, nor is it transformed by Prospero's magic, which uses nature to create certain illusions, but does not bring the Golden Age to his temporary abode. In this way the island in *The Tempest* allows the audience to understand the mystification of nature in the islands of the court masques, in the Stuart rhetoric, with its echoes in *Cymbeline*. Prospero's island may make his magical control of the space more credible, but it does not show him transforming nature as does the king in *Oberon*.

Prospero's magic, although it invites comparison with powers attributed to James in the masques, is really more comparable to that of the masque-maker than the ruler for whom the masque was created. Prospero is the master of the illusion of power, and by making the ruler his own masque-maker Shakespeare enables his audience to see the ruler's use of art to control others: he exposes the ideology of art.

Although Prospero gives the audience a hyperbolic sense of his own power in the abjuration speech, as we have said, much of the action of the play exposes the limits of his power. Caliban proves impervious to nurture, using language to curse, yet chafing at his colonized status. He is hardly the happy subject of a benevolent nourish-father. Ariel, too, longs for his freedom, for Prospero's magic has released him from the tree prison to another bondage. Ariel's banquet has a definite effect on Alonso, but Antonio's silence suggests little repentence or regeneration. Prospero's masterpiece, the wedding masque, is abridged, just at the moment of controlling the seasons, by the prospect of conspiracy and mortality. Prospero's art seems full of power at first, but its limits in governing a variety of creatures are gradually revealed.[124] The only subjects who respond well to it are the naturally noble: Miranda, Ferdinand, Alonso, Gonzalo, all born as much to govern as to be governed.

In fact, *The Tempest* implies that Prospero's greatest temptation as a ruler is his imitation of the role of the ruler in a Jonsonian masque. Control of illusion has become the illusion of control. He has become dependent on the "fantasy of omnipotence" given him by control of the island through his magic. Because that god-like power is an illusion, a political myth, Prospero must learn to govern himself in the presence of the unregenerate and the gentle alike. He must free both Ariel and Caliban. He must control his rage at imperfection and at his own mortality, the ultimate subject of illusion for the god-like. As he acknowledges his beating mind to Ferdinand or claims Caliban as his own, we sense that he is moving away, not just from tyranny, but from the god-like conception of the ruler in Stuart ideology. Self-governance, that old-fashioned ideal of the books for princes, will pierce the illusion of god-like power.[125]

Prospero has a human, if not humane, conception of himself as ruler as he departs for the ambiguous and ordinary dukedom in Milan. He demonstrates this less by abjuring the magic which originally drew him away from politics than by acknowledging the power of the audience in the epilogue. Prospero puts the audience in precisely his place during the play, and just as he has freed Ariel, so the power of their imaginations will perform for him what his magic has done before. The audience must not bind him to the bare island by a spell as Sycorax imprisoned Ariel in a tree, but their hands must release the suppliant:

> Gentle breath of yours my sails
> Must fill, or else my project fails,
> Which was to please. Now I want
> Spirits to enforce, art to enchant,
> And my ending is despair,
> Unless I be reliev'd by prayer,
> Which pierces so that it assaults
> Mercy itself and frees all faults.
> As you from crimes would pardon'd be,
> Let your indulgence set me free.
> (5.Epilogue.11–20)

The consummate illusionist acknowledges that much of the power of all art lies in the beholder, a gesture in which *The Tempest* reveals its affinity with the court masque and its critique of the Stuart ideology. Shakespeare is gracefully using the familiar pretense that the ruler brings into existence any productions performed before him: "His presence gives them life; his absence robs them. Their existence depends on him."[126] When *The Tempest* was performed at court, the most important member of the audience could indeed believe that his breath would fill sails. Yet, paradoxically, the representation of kingly power without the illusionist's art is limited indeed. One is tempted to say that there is more power in the illusion than in the ruler.

If we read back from *The Tempest* to the earlier romances, we may now understand their emphatic reminders that they are artistic constructs. The self-consciousness of *Pericles, Cymbeline,* and *The Winter's Tale* alerts the audience to the process which *The Tempest* exposes: art using nature to mythologize power. The more aware the audience becomes that it is watching a work of art, the more conscious it will be that what is made to seem natural and inevitable is really artifice conforming to human authority. The development of this self-consciousness on the part of the audience of the romances brings together characteristics of the plays not usually linked. The old-fashioned genre of romance insists upon that awareness, but even if we are insensitive to that fact, each play contains elements which tell the audience that they are watching illusion. In *Pericles* we have Gower resurrected to frame events which happened in the antique past, to be told in the Middle Ages, and now retold: "To sing a song that old was sung, / From ashes ancient Gower is come" (1.1.1–2). Similar elements appear in *The Winter's Tale* where the bear, the figure of Time, the echoes of the title, and the statue insist "that a tale is not life but an image of life."[127] The tendency of *Cymbeline* to call attention to its own theatrical virtuosity has been thoroughly explored by Arthur Kirsch and Roger Warren.[128] Both critics accent the three most remarkable loci for this effect: Imogen's waking by Cloten's corpse, the descent of Jupiter in Posthumus's dream, and Iachimo's behavior in Imogen's chamber. Both critics stress the variety of often contradictory emotions evoked in both character and audience by these scenes. As Warren says, "In each of the central scenes, theatrical virtuosity on an elaborate scale is set off against language of great simplicity or emotional intensity or both." Kirsch emphasizes the misunderstandings, such as those attached to the death of Imogen disguised as Fidele, which make the audience self-conscious about its own emotions with regard to the experience represented in the play.[129] These contradictions are so marked, in fact, that two recent critics have called *Cymbeline* a parodic drama.[130]

William Matchett has written in a similar way of *The Winter's Tale,* calling attention to the tragic elements of the action, such as the death of Mamillius, in a framing romantic action: "No simple response is adequate and we are left shaken not only by tragedy but by the necessity of continuing to respond after that pattern had appeared complete." Matchett also suggests that inappropriate elements, such as the conventional matching of Camillo and Paulina at the last minute, "bring us back to the stage." This awareness of the play itself allows the audience to understand both the illusion and the nature of it: "the gain in calling attention to the fact is that breaking in upon the illusion allows a fuller comprehension."[131] I would add that this comprehension allows the audience to perceive the self-correcting devices of the romance, such as the substitution of Florizel for Mamillius, against the theme of nature's triumph over art. The effect allows the audience to become skeptical about a highly artificial genre which seeks to ground itself in nature. This technique becomes, as we have said, a theme in *The Tempest,* where Prospero seems to control nature by manipulating human perceptions of it. By introducing these dramaturgic effects and this theme of illusion into plays which mythologize their patriarchal structures as natural and inevitable, pure and simple, Shakespeare enables his audience to recognize political ideology in its literary representation.

EPILOGUE

This analysis of the three eras of Shake-
speare's comedies demonstrates the usefulness of approaching them through the theories of Michael Foucault, especially those in *The History of Sexuality*. As Foucault has taught us,
the fact that comedies are about love and personal themes
does not preclude their also being about power. Foucault
insisted that we revise our ideas about power and sex: "We
must at the same time conceive of sex without the law, and
power without the king." As we saw in the Introduction, for
Foucault power was neither an institution nor a structure.
Having reviewed the eleven comedies that form the subject
of this study, we are in a good position to give assent to
Foucault's generalization:

> It seems to me that power must be understood in the first
> instance as the multiplicity of force relations immanent in the
> sphere in which they operate and which constitute their own

177

organization; as the process which, through ceaseless struggles and confrontations, transforms, strengthens, or reverses
them; as the support which these force relations find in one
another, thus forming a chain or system, or on the contrary,
the disjunctions and contradictions which isolate them from
one another; and lastly, as the strategies in which they take
effect, whose general design or institutional crystallization is
embodied in the state apparatus, in the formulation of the
law, in the various social hegemonies.

This definition is particularly useful in understanding the
sexual politics of the comedies beyond the varied social
structures in which they represent the patriarchy. One perceives why the desire of men may never be constrained without rebellion, why women's power is transgressive unless
gained through suffering, why daughters and not sons redeem their fathers. In comedies as in history, power is hidden: "Power is tolerable only on condition that it mask a
substantial part of itself. Its success is proportional to its ability to hide its own mechanisms."[1] The truth of this generalization is apparent not just in the disguises of Vincentio or
Polixenes, but in the idealization of women in the romantic
comedies and the romances, a valuation that masks their use
as objects of exchange among men or the simple disap-
pearance of their generativity (Hermione or Thaisa). Moreover, Portia is one of the most skillful disguisers of power in
dramatic literature.

Significant for feminists today are the ways in which
Shakespeare represents but also masks the imperative of
male control over female sexuality and generativity. Two sets
of plays turn the issue into a sexual one: the romantic comedies see all men as rivals, and so they are preoccupied with
women as property in marriage and with cuckoldry. The
problem plays turn issues of bastardy (*Measure*) and alliance
(*All's Well*) into bed tricks at the command of the male. The
romances mythologize the father as totally responsible for
procreation of his family. It is instructive to observe how little
the issues of control of female sexuality and reproduction
have changed from Shakespeare's time to ours, despite the

decline in the importance of alliance and the development of new technologies in birth control and abortion. Had Foucault finished *The History of Sexuality,* he might have discovered this pattern.

Foucault thought that sex was created by sexuality:

> We must not make the mistake of thinking that sex is an autonomous agency which secondarily produces manifold effects of sexuality over the entire length of its surface of contact with power. On the contrary, sex is the most speculative, most ideal, and most internal element in a deployment of sexuality organized by power in its grip on bodies and their materiality, their forces, energies, sensations, and pleasures.

The change in notions of sex from the Petrarchan discourse of the romantic comedies to the problem plays affords a vivid example of this formulation. The Petrarchan structures identify the lady with all that man desires: wealth, position, lineage. In this discourse, sex is literally worth dying for.[2] The comedies do not require this sacrifice, but *Romeo and Juliet,* written in the same discourse, does. Rosalind may be skeptical about these ideals: "But these are all lies: men have died from time to time and worms have eaten them, but not for love" (4.1.106–8), but her momentary contradiction only reinforces the general impression of *As You Like It* that sex is a wondrous good of life. When, however, history empties meaning from the Petrarchan structures on which this discourse depends, sex becomes a hunger that consumes males, as in Claudio's remark to Lucio: "Our nature do pursue / Like rats that ravin down their proper bane, / A thirsty evil; and when we drink we die" (1.11.132–34). Gone is the idealization of women as identified with all men desire; women become, instead, "rotten medlars." These changes come about when social conditions have deprived women of their symbolic power, and male desire now conflicts with male power.

The central core of Foucault's argument that has been useful in this book is that sex is created by sexuality and that sexuality is a historical construct:

> Sexuality must not be thought of as a kind of natural given which power tries to hold in check, or as an obscure domain which knowledge tries gradually to uncover. It is the name that can be given to a historical construct: not a furtive reality that is difficult to grasp, but a great surface network in which the stimulation of bodies, the intensification of pleasures, the incitement to discourse, the formation of special knowledges, the strengthening of controls and resistances, are linked to one another, in accordance with a few major strategies of knowledge and power.[3]

In any period, then, sexuality is a set of effects, not a cause of behavior, derived from a nexus of social, political, and economic conditions. This is why there are class sexualities, such as those in *As You Like It* or *Measure*. The sexuality of *Much Ado,* with its distinctive lack of trust, may also be seen as a class phenomenon.

If we understand sexuality as an instrument of power's design, we must ask ourselves about the kinds of power a society can exercise with regard to sexuality. The law was far too simple for Foucault or, indeed, all forms of power that are negative and threaten life. Instead, the power appropriate to sexuality is regulatory and corrective:

> The law always refers to the sword. But the power whose task is to take charge of life needs continuous regulatory and corrective mechanisms. It is no longer a matter of bringing death into play in the field of sovereignty, but of distributing the living in the domain of value and utility. Such a power has to qualify, measure, appraise, and hierarchize, rather than display itself in its murderous splendor; it does not have to draw the line that separates the enemies of the sovereign from his obedient subjects; it effects distributions around the norm.[4]

Such a power uses surveillance and various forms of management of the body. We have seen in *Measure* the surveillance of the disguised ruler, a Renaissance Panopticon: the subjects' transgressions are visible to the invisible ruler.[5] Polixenes at the sheepshearing in *Winter's Tale* and the spying parents of the enforced-marriage plays are similar figures. Shakespeare agrees with Foucault by implying in *Measure* that the Duke's life-and-death power is inappropriate and ineffectual in dealing with sexuality. Instead Vincentio resorts to the surveillance and intervention Foucault highlights; Vincentio's power is the covert management of human lives under the authority of religion. *Measure* with its images of confined spaces, such as the immured garden and the moated grange, anticipates in an uncanny way Foucault's comments on the orderings of space that are part of a "whole series of different tactics that combined in varying proportions the objective of disciplining the body and that of regulating populations."[6]

Alliance, "a system of marriage, of fixation and deployment of kinship ties, of transmission of name and possessions," is important in the societies Shakespeare represents in his comedies. These considerations are invariably present in the frames of the romantic comedies, where the terms of Portia's father's will in *Merchant,* the conflicts between brothers in *As You Like It,* the deaths of Olivia's father and brother in *Twelfth Night,* and the behavior of Leonato in *Much Ado* form the basic premises on which the romantic comedies operate. Bertram's status as ward to the king and his lineage are crucial elements in *All's Well,* where Helena's getting pregnant by Bertram and her possession of his monumental ring are symbolic elements in their reconciliation. Foucault observes that in societies of alliance the family is "the interchange of sexuality and alliance: it conveys the law and the juridical dimension in the deployment of sexuality; and it conveys the economy of pleasure and the intensity of sensations in the regime of alliance."[7] Among Shakespeare's comedies, the romances best illustrate this effect. The dispersal and reunion of the family of the ruler provides the realm with the needed heirs, a process by which their sexuality is largely defined and which is inscribed in nature. Shakespeare's device of fusing the figures of ruler and father in both the problem plays and the romances allows him to represent patriarchal power as entirely natural. Here we should observe that although for the romances the deployment of alliance virtually supplanted the deployment of sexuality, in our own time sexuality has almost entirely supplanted alliance, largely because inherited wealth is a relatively small factor in contemporary society.[8] Yet we observe that many of the imperatives about the control of female reproduction thought necessary in structures of alliance are still with us, somewhat transformed, but with us still. Their endurance may be partly the result of assumptions about nature as a basis for social structures, as implied in the romances.

If Foucault is immensely useful in reading Shakespeare's comedies, study of Shakespeare also may lead us to modify Foucault's theories with evidence from the plays and their historical context. Although Foucault emphasizes the notion of sexuality as a historical construct, his descriptions of historical change are too glacial for agreement with the rate of change in Shakespeare's work. The three kinds of comedy studied here were composed and produced within less than two decades, from about 1594–95 to about 1612. This suggests that the widely differing concepts of sexuality which we have found in the romantic comedies and the problem plays especially, coexisted within English society of the time and that the particular structures and discourse adopted in a genre made use of one or another notion of sexuality, depending upon relatively specific conditions. The long reign of Elizabeth I certainly gave vitality to the Petrarchan discourse of the romantic comedies, yet the themes of enforced marriage and sexual nausea can be found in English literature for years before 1603. What the comedies demonstrate, then, is that in sexuality as in all other cultural constructs, societies are not monologic, but full of ideas, some old or new, some dying and some just born. When the Stuarts revived the old patriarchal ideology, held in abeyance by the presence of a female ruler, Shakespeare could revive the old romance genre with its use of nature and capacity to mythologize the political ideology. Doubtless, if he had lived to finish *The History of Sexuality*, Foucault would have made similar discoveries. It is, however, a significant refinement on the notion that sexuality is historically contingent.

As we observed earlier, another term that has been crucial in the argument of this study is nature, which, we have observed, is also historically contingent and which even changes from one romance to another. Yet, understanding of the way nature operates to mythologize power in the romances is significant for contemporary feminists. Concepts of what is natural have been used to coerce and oppress women, minorities, and sexual deviants throughout history. Whether the argument is based on size or strength or intelligence, the appeal is basically similar: inferiority is immutable because it is grounded in nature and not socially constructed. Similarly, the sexually deviant are held to nature as normative. Yet what we learn from the romances is that nature, like sexuality, is a historical construct. Because the romances mythologize a distinct political ideology that we can analyze historically, they help us see how subtle these assumptions about nature can be and how a political regime may use them to oppose the growth of ideas that may provide for social change, in this case, those of the contractualists. The fact that the Stuarts were using old-fashioned ideas for a losing struggle should not lead us to dismiss their attempt to make a particular political structure seem permanent. Instead, such knowledge is empowering to women, minorities, and sexual deviants, for whenever the opponents of their interests begin to argue from concepts of nature, they, like the Stuarts, may be attempting to make the historically contingent seem unchangeable. The social constructs human beings invent, they may also change.

ℵOTES

Introduction

1. See, for example, Elizabeth Janeway, *Powers of the Weak* (New York: Knopf, 1980).
2. Michel Foucault, *Power/Knowledge: Selected Interviews and Other Writings 1972–1977*, ed. Colin Gordon, trans. Colin Gordon, Leo Marshall, John Mepham, and Kate Soper (New York: Pantheon, 1980), p. 98.
3. Jean Bodin says, "as much as that libertie which nature hath given unto every one to live at his owne pleasure, bound within no lawes, is yet subiecte unto the ruler and power of some other. All which power to commaund over others, is either publick or privat," in *The Six Bookes of a Commonweale*, ed. K. D. McRae, Facsimile of English Translation of 1606 (Cambridge, Mass.: Harvard University Press, 1962), p. 14.
4. Stephen Greenblatt, Introduction to *The Power of Forms in the English Renaissance* (Norman, Okla.: Pilgrim Books, 1982).
5. Lawrence Stone, "Social Mobility in England, 1500–1700," *Seventeenth-Century England: Society in an Age of Revolution,* ed. Paul Seaver (New York: Franklin Watts, 1976), pp. 26–50.
6. Lawrence Stone, *Family, Sex and Marriage in England 1500–1800* (New York: Harper and Row, 1977), and for some correction of Stone's views, Keith Wrightson, *English Society 1580–1680* (New Brunswick, N.J.: Rutgers University Press, 1982).
7. See, for example, Linda Woodbridge, *Women and the English Renaissance: Literature and the Nature of Womankind, 1540–1640* (Urbana, Ill.: University of Illinois Press, 1984).

185

8. For an excellent summary of this complex subject, see Catherine Belsey, *Critical Practice* (London: Methuen, 1980), pp. 37–47, and Josue V. Harari, "Critical Factions/Critical Fictions," *Textual Strategies: Perspectives in Post-Structuralist Criticism* (Ithaca, N.Y.: Cornell University Press, 1979). More thorough and provocative is Michel Foucault, *The Order of Things: An Archaeology of the Human Sciences* (New York: Vintage Books, 1970), chap. 3, "Representing," and chap. 7, "The Limits of Representation."

9. See Belsey, *Critical Practice*, pp. 56–90, and Jonathan Dollimore, *Radical Tragedy: Religion, Ideology and Power in the Drama of Shakespeare and His Contemporaries* (Chicago, Ill.: University of Chicago Press, 1984), pp. 9–19. In back of this thinking lies the work of Louis Althusser in *For Marx*, trans. Ben Brewster (London: New Left Books, 1977), and *Lenin and Philosophy and Other Essays*, trans. Ben Brewster (London: New Left Books, 1977); for a critique of Althusser, see E. P. Thompson, *The Poverty of Theory and Other Essays* (New York: Monthly Review Press, 1978).

10. See Dollimore, *Radical Tragedy*, pp. 11–19.

11. Stephen Greenblatt, *Renaissance Self-Fashioning from More to Shakespeare* (Chicago, Ill.: University of Chicago Press, 1980), p. 5.

12. Natalie Zemon Davis, "Women on Top," *Society and Culture in Early Modern France* (Stanford, Calif.: Stanford University Press, 1975), chap. 5.

13. Jonathan Goldberg, *James I and the Politics of Literature: Jonson, Shakespeare, Donne, and Their Contemporaries* (Baltimore, Md.: Johns Hopkins University Press, 1983).

14. Belsey, *Critical Practice*, p. 109.

15. Louis Adrian Montrose, " 'Shaping Fantasies': Figurations of Gender and Power in Elizabethan Culture," *Representations* 2 (1983): 61–94.

16. Juliet Dusinberre, *Shakespeare and the Nature of Women* (New York: Harper and Row, 1975).

17. Irene Dash, *Wooing, Wedding, and Power: Women in Shakespeare's Plays* (New York: Columbia University Press, 1981), p. 6.

18. Marilyn French, *Shakespeare's Division of Experience* (New York: Summit Books, 1981); Linda Bamber, *Comic Women, Tragic Men: A Study of Gender and Genre in Shakespeare* (Stanford, Calif.: Stanford University Press, 1982).

19. Coppelia Kahn, *Man's Estate: Masculine Identity in Shakespeare* (Berkeley, Calif.: University of California Press, 1981), p. 12.

20. Lisa Jardine, *Still Harping on Daughters: Women and Drama in the Age of Shakespeare* (Sussex: Harvester Press, 1983), p. 7.

21. Veronica Beechey, "On Patriarchy," *Feminist Review* 3 (1979): 67, 80.

22. See Gordon Schochet, *Patriarchalism in Political Thought: The Authoritarian Family and Political Speculation and Attitudes Especially in Seventeenth-Century England* (Oxford: Blackwell, 1975).

23. Stephen Orgel, *The Illusion of Power: Political Theater in the English Renaissance* (Berkeley, Calif.: University of California Press, 1975); *Patronage in the Renaissance*, ed. Guy Fitch Lytle and Stephen Orgel (Princeton, N.J.: Princeton University Press, 1981); for *Power of Forms*, see n. 4; for *James I*, see n. 13; Louis Adrian Montrose, " 'Eliza, Queene of the Shepheardes' and the Pastoral of Power," *ELR* 10 (1980): 153–82. See also two review articles by Jonathan Goldberg: "The Politics of Renaissance Literature: A Review Essay," *ELH* 49 (1982): 514–42, and "Recent Studies in the English Renaissance," *SEL* 24 (1984): 157–99.

24. Coppelia Kahn pointed to this gap at the Shakespeare Association of America Convention in April 1984. Her work, like that of Peter Erickson, deals with patriarchal structures through psychoanalytic models combined with cultural codes.

25. Bamber, *Comic Women*, p. 21.

26. Arthur Marotti, "'Love Is Not Love': Elizabethan Sonnet Sequences and the Social Order," *ELH* 49 (1982): 396–428.
27. Anthony Esler, *The Aspiring Mind of the Elizabethan Younger Generation* (Durham, N.C.: Duke University Press, 1966).
28. F. E. Halliday, *A Shakespeare Companion 1564–1964* (Harmondsworth, Middlesex: Penguin Books, 1964), p. 94.
29. Allison Heisch, "Queen Elizabeth I and the Persistence of Patriarchy," *Feminist Review* 4 (1980): 45–56.

Chapter One

1. All references to Shakespeare's plays are to *The Complete Works of Shakespeare*, ed. David Bevington, 3d ed. (Glenview: Ill.: Scott, Foresman, 1980).
2. Arthur F. Marotti, "'Love Is Not Love': Elizabethan Sonnet Sequences and the Social Order," *ELH* 49 (1982): 398.
3. Herbert Moller, "The Social Causation of the Courtly Love Complex," *Comparative Studies in History and Society* 1 (1958–59): 137–59, and "The Meaning of Courtly Love," *Journal of American Folklore* 73 (1960): 39–52.
4. Georges Duby, *Medieval Marriage: Two Models from Twelfth-Century France*, trans. Elborg Foster (Baltimore, Md.: Johns Hopkins University Press, 1978), pp. 10–14.
5. Barnaby Barnes, sonnet xx, *Parthenophil and Parthenophe* (1593) in *Elizabethan Sonnets*, ed. Sidney Lee (English Garner, 1904; reprint, New York: Cooper Square, 1964), 1:181.
6. *Ibid.*, 1:232.
7. Sir Philip Sidney, *Fifth Song* in *ibid.*, 1:73.
8. Samuel Daniel, sonnet xxvii, *Delia* (1592) in *ibid.*, 1:102.
9. Edward DeVere, Earl of Oxford, *Megliora Spero* (1591) in *ibid.*, 1:107.
10. Wallace MacCaffrey, "Place and Patronage in Elizabethan Politics," *Elizabethan Government and Society: Essays Presented to Sir John Neale*, ed. S. T. Bindoff, Joel Hurstfield, and C. H. Williams (London: Athlone Press, 1961), pp. 95–126; Lawrence Stone, *The Crisis of the Aristocracy: 1558–1641* (Oxford: Clarendon Press, 1965), pp. 385–504.
11. Barnes, canzon 2, *Parthenophil and Parthenophe* (1593) in *Sonnets*, ed. Lee, 1:273.
12. Leonard Foster, *The Icy Fire: Five Studies of European Petrarchism* (Cambridge: Cambridge University Press, 1969), pp. 122–47; Roy Strong, *The Cult of Elizabeth: Elizabethan Portraiture and Pagentry* (London: Thames and Hudson, 1977); Louis A. Montrose, "Celebration and Insinuation: Sir Philip Sidney and the Motives of Elizabethan Courtship," *Renaissance Drama* n.s. 8 (1977): 3–35.
13. Marotti, "Love," pp. 398–99.
14. Joel Fineman, "Fratricide and Cuckoldry: Shakespeare's Doubles," *Representing Shakespeare: New Psychoanalytic Essays*, ed. Murray Schwartz and Coppelia Kahn (Baltimore, Md.: Johns Hopkins University Press, 1980), p. 80.
15. Richard Helgerson, *The Elizabethan Prodigals* (Berkeley, Calif.: University of California Press, 1976), pp. 41–42.
16. E. Pearlman, "Shakespeare, Freud, and the Two Usuries, or, Money's Medlar," *ELR* 2 (1972): 217–36.
17. Louis A. Montrose, "'The Place of a Brother' in *As You Like It:* Social Process and Comic Form," *SQ* 32 (1981): 28–54.
18. *Ibid.*, pp. 50–51.
19. Lawrence Stone, "Social Mobility in England, 1500–1700," *Seventeenth-Century England: Society in an Age of Revolution*, ed. Paul Seaver (New York: Franklin Watts, 1976), p. 43.

20. Peter Laslett, *The World We Have Lost,* 2d ed. (New York: Scribners, 1973), p. 39.
21. Stone, "Social Mobility," p. 43.
22. Marotti, "Love," p. 416.
23. Anthony Esler, *The Aspiring Mind of the Elizbethan Younger Generation* (Durham, N.C.: Duke University Press, 1966), pp. 51–86.
24. See Helgerson, *Prodigals,* pp. 23–30; Esler, *Generation,* pp. 125–64; Lawrence Stone, "The Educational Revolution in England, 1560–1640," *Past and Present* 28 (1964): 41–80.
25. Mark Curtis, "The Alienated Intellectuals of Early Stuart England," *Past and Present* 23 (1962): 25–41.
26. Laslett, *World,* pp. 11–12.
27. *Ibid.,* p. 48.
28. John Aylmer, *An Harborowe for Faithful and Trewe Subiectes, agaynst the Late Blowne Blaste, concerninge the Governmet of Women,* quoted by Carroll Camden in *The Elizabethan Woman* (Houston, Tex.: Elsevier Press, 1952), p. 254.
29. See Kathleen M. Davies, "The Sacred Condition of Equality—How Original Were Puritan Doctrines of Marriage?" *Social History* 5 (1977): 563–80.
30. Ian Maclean, *The Renaissance Notion of Woman* (Cambridge: Cambridge University Press, 1980), pp. 84–85.
31. Ruth Kelso, *Doctrine for the Lady of the Renaissance* (Urbana, Ill.: University of Illinois Press, 1956), p. 273.
32. Jessie Bernard, *The Future of Marriage* (New York: Bantam Books, 1973).
33. For an opposing view, see Lisa Jardine, *Still Harping on Daughters* (Sussex: Harvester Press, 1983), pp. 103–40. Harry Berger sees Portia as manipulative in the casket scene and using devices—negative usury, "mercifixion," and the charity that wounds to control Bassanio and herself in "Marriage and Mercifixion in *The Merchant of Venice,*" *SQ* 32 (1981): 155–62.
34. Coppelia Kahn, *Man's Estate: Masculine Identity in Shakespeare* (Berkeley, Calif.: University of California Press, 1981), p. 150.
35. See L. T. Fitz, "'What Says the Married Woman?': Marriage Theory and Feminism in the English Renaissance," *Mosaic* 13 (1980): 1–22; Camden, *Elizabethan Woman,* pp. 17–35; L. B. Wright, *Middle-Class Culture in Elizabethan England* (Chapel Hill, N.C.: University of North Carolina Press, 1935), pp. 465–507.
36. *England as seen by Foreigners in the Days of Elizabeth and James the First,* ed. W. B. Rye (1865; reprint, New York: Benjamin Blom, 1967), p. 7.
37. Fitz, "Married Woman," p. 12.
38. See Camden, *Elizabethan Woman,* pp. 241–71.
39. F. G. Emmison, *Elizabethan Life: Morals and the Church Courts* (Chelmsford: Essex County Council, 1970), p. 18. He cites six instances from 1585 to 1595. For discussion of the later controversy in James's time, see Wright, *Middle-Class Culture,* pp. 494–502; Fitz, "Married Woman," pp. 15–17; and Jardine, *Daughters,* pp. 93–98. A complete review of the whole issue is now available in Linda Woodbridge, *Women and the English Renaissance* (Urbana, Ill.: University of Illinois Press, 1984), pp. 139–83.
40. *Hic Mulier; or The Man-Woman: Being a Medicine to cure the Coltish Disease of the Staggers in the Masculine-Femines of our Times* (London: G. Purslowe for J. Trundle, 1620), Sig. A3.
41. See W. C. Hazlitt, *Faiths and Folkore of the British Isles* (1905; reprint, New York: Benjamin Blom, 1965), pp. 159–62; *Cuckolds, Clerics, and Countrymen: Medieval French Fabliaux,* trans. and ed. John DuVal and Raymond Eichman (Fayetteville, Ark.: University of Arkansas Press, 1982); and *Shakespeare Jest Books,* ed. W. C. Hazlitt, 3 vols. (London: Willis and Sothernam, 1864).
42. Kahn, *Man's Estate,* p. 121.
43. From *Certayne Conceyts & Jests* in *Shakespeare Jest Books,* ed. Hazlitt, 3:27.

44. *Cuckolds,* ed. DuVal and Eichman, p. 9.
45. Nahum Tate, *Cuckolds-Haven: or an Alderman no Conjurer* (London: Edward Poole, 1685), p. 44.
46. Ben Jonson, George Chapman, and John Marston, *Eastward Ho!,* ed. C. G. Petter (London: Ernest Benn, 1973), 5.5.177.
47. Natalie Zemon Davis, "Women on Top," *Society and Culture in Early Modern France* (Stanford, Calif.: Stanford University Press, 1975), p. 134.
48. F. P. Wilson, ed., *The Batchelars Banquet* (Oxford: Clarendon, 1929), pp. xxiii–xxxv.
49. In *Shakespeare Jest Books,* ed. Hazlitt, vol. 3.
50. Davis, "Women on Top," pp. 134–35.
51. Paul Hair, ed., *Before the Bawdy Court* (London: Paul Elek, 1972), says "the judgment in adultery cases normally included a warning that the parties were to keep apart in future. It is noticeable that, while fornication was regarded by many as barely an offence, no-one made any defence of adultery (even though there was considerable moral justification for some of the irregular unions)" (p. 236).
52. F. G. Emmison, *Elizabethan Life: Disorder* (Chelmsford: Essex County Council, 1970), pp. 69–74.
53. Emmison, *Morals,* p. 54.
54. Emmison, *Disorder,* p. 68.
55. As in *De la Saineresse* in *Cuckolds,* ed. DuVal and Eichman.
56. As in the ballad "Old Wicket" in *Ancient Poems, Ballads, and Songs of the Peasantry of England,* ed. J. H. Dixon (1846; reprint, Menston: Scholar Press, 1973), pp. 212–14.
57. Quoted by Hazlitt, *Folklore,* p. 161. See Emmison, *Disorder,* p. 69. For a map of the haven's location, see Appendix 1 in *Eastward Ho!,* ed. Petter, pp. 120–21.
58. Davis, "Women on Top," p. 135.
59. Kahn, *Man's Estate,* p. 150.
60. The joke is called Hans Carvel's Ring, and it was widely used in the Renaissance by Rabelais, Erasmus, and Poggio. A version of it appears in *Mery Tales and Quicke Answeres* in *Shakespeare Jest Books,* ed. Hazlitt, 1:28: "A man that was ryght iolous on his wyfe, dreamed on a nyght as he laye a bed with her and slepte, that the dyvell aperd unto him and sayde: woldest thou not be gladde that I shulde put thee in suretie of thy wife? Yes, sayde he. Holde, sayde the dyvell, as long as thou hast this rynge upon thy fynger, no man shall make thee kockolde. The man was gladde thereof, and when he awaked, he founde his fynger in * * *." See Marilyn Williamson, "The Ring Episode in *The Merchant of Venice,*" *SAQ* 71 (1972): 587–94, and Anne Parten, "Re-establishing Sexual Order: The Ring Episode in *The Merchant of Venice,*" *Women's Studies* 9 (1982): 145–55. Parten sees Portia as rejecting the cuckoldry theme and becoming the ideal wife in a marriage no longer threatened by her strength and feats while in disguise. Clearly I disagree.
61. Keith Thomas, "The Place of Laughter in Tudor and Stuart England," *Times Literary Supplement,* 21 January 1977, p. 77.
62. Davis, "Women on Top," p. 131.

Chapter Two

1. F. E. Halliday, *A Shakespeare Companion 1564–1964* (Harmondsworth: Penguin Books, 1964), p. 93.
2. *The Basilicon Doron of James VI,* ed. James Craigie (Edinburgh: Blackwood, 1944), 1:55, 81, 115.

3. Lawrence Stone, *Family, Sex and Marriage in England 1500–1800* (New York: Harper and Row, 1977), p. 218.

4. Lawrence Stone, "Social Mobility in England, 1500–1700," *Seventeenth-Century England: Society in an Age of Revolution,* ed. Paul Seaver (New York: Franklin Watts, 1976), pp. 42–43.

5. Lawrence Stone, "The Educational Revolution in England, 1560–1640," *Past and Present* 28 (1964): 68–70.

6. All documentation for this complex argument is cited in the discussion of *Measure*.

7. Michel Foucault, *The History of Sexuality*, trans. Robert Hurley (New York: Vintage Books, 1980), pp. 25–26.

8. Shakespeare's use of the bed trick is acknowledged to be unusual by Rosalind Miles, *The Problem of "Measure for Measure": A Historical Investigation* (New York: Barnes and Noble, 1976), pp. 236–46.

9. Glenn H. Blayney, "The Enforcement of Marriage in English Drama 1600–1650," *PQ* 38 (1959): 469.

10. Quoted in Blayney, "Enforcement," p. 469.

11. Thomas Dekker, *Seven Deadly Sins of London* in *The Non-Dramatic Works,* ed. A. B. Grosart (1885; reprint, New York: Russell and Russell, 1963), 2:70–72; Barnaby Rich, *Faultes Faults and Nothing Else But Faultes,* ed. M. H. Wolf (Gainesville, Fla.: Scholars Facsimiles and Reprints, 1965), pp. 26ff; Heywood is quoted in Blayney, "Enforcement," p. 471.

12. Thomas Gataker, *A Good Wife Gods Gift: and A Wife Indeed Two Marriage Sermons* (London: Printed by John Haviland for Fulke Clifton, 1623), p. 11.

13. William Gouge, *Of Domestical Duties* (London: Printed by I. Haviland for W. Braden, 1622), p. 585, and William Perkins, *Christian Oeconomie,* trans. T. Pickering (London: E. Weaver, 1609), sig. Fi.

14. George Whetstone, *An Heptameron of Civill Discourses* (London: Richard Jones, 1582), Sig. Flr.

15. See Margot Heinemann, who says, "Middleton's city comedies, like much of the major drama of the period, present a society changing from one regulated by inherited status to one ruled increasingly by the power of money and capital, with much greater social mobility, and hence with an increasing sense of opportunity and insecurity" (*Puritanism and Theatre: Thomas Middleton and Opposition Drama and the Early Stuarts* [Cambridge: Cambridge University Press, 1980], p. 66).

16. "The land-owning classes, well represented in the House of Commons, had celebrated the arrival of the new king with a strong demand that the long standing abuse of wardship should be dealth with once for all" (Joel Hurstfield, *The Queen's Wards: Wardship and Marriage under Elizabeth I,* 2d ed. [London: Frank Cass, 1973], p. 315).

17. See H. E. Bell, *An Introduction to the History and Records of the Court of Wards and Liveries* (Cambridge: Cambridge University Press, 1953), pp. 1–15.

18. *Ibid.,* p. 125.

19. *Ibid.,* p. 126; see also Hurstfield, *Wards,* chap. 8, "Marriage."

20. Sir Thomas Smith, *De Republica Anglorum,* ed. Mary Dewar (Cambridge: Cambridge University Press, 1982), p. 87.

21. *The Political Works of James I,* ed. C. H. McIlwain (Cambridge, Mass.: Harvard University Press, 1918), p. 36.

22. Smith, *De Republica,* pp. 128–29.

23. See Bell, *Introduction,* pp. 114–15; Hurstfield, *Wards,* pp. 181–217; Glenn Blayney, "Wardship in English Drama (1600–1650)," *SP* 53 (1956): 471.

24. *The London Prodigal,* ed. Edmond Malone (London: C. Bathurst, 1780); *The Miseries of Enforced Marriage,* ed. Glenn Blayney, Malone Society Reprint (Oxford: Oxford University Press, 1963); *The Yorkshire Tragedy,* ed. Edmond Mal-

one (London: C. Bathurst, 1780); *How a Man May Choose a Good Wife from a Bad,* ed. A. E. H. Swaen (Louvain: A. Uystpruyst, 1912); *The Honest Whore, The Dramatic Works of Thomas Dekker,* ed. Fredson Bowers (Cambridge: Cambridge University Press, 1953–70).

25. Richard Helgerson, *The Elizabethan Prodigals* (Berkeley, Calif.: University of California Press, 1976).

26. *Ibid.,* p. 35.

27. Richard Wever, *Lusty Juventus, The Dramatic Writings of Richard Wever and Thomas Ingelend,* ed. J. S. Farmer (1905; reprint, New York: Barnes and Noble, 1966), pp. 36–37.

28. *Ibid.,* p. 90.

29. *Narrative and Dramatic Sources of Shakespeare,* ed. Geoffrey Bullough (London: Routledge and Kegan Paul, 1958), 2:391.

30. *Misogonus, Six Anonymous Plays,* ed. J. S. Farmer (1906; reprint, New York: Barnes and Noble, 1958), 2:391.

31. Helgerson, *Prodigal,* p. 35.

32. Edited by H. B. Wheatley (London: Villon Society, 1855).

33. Giovanni Boccaccio, *The Decameron,* trans. John Payne (New York: World Publishing, 1947), p. 687.

34. Howard C. Cole reads Helena as a self-deceived deceiver, manipulative, but naive about her own motives: "Regarded without reference to her sisters' pious deceits, Helena's manipulations of truths into illusions and people into puppets have been viewed as intimations of two of her more powerful though radically different successors, either the 'fantastical Duke of dark corners' . . . or the far more sympathetic Prospero. . . . The All's Well story, on the other hand, encourages us to look for duplicities we may not be able to prove, a heroine who is a self-deceived deceiver, intriguing as shrewdly as a ruthless Vincentio while honestly seeing herself as a benevolent Prospero" (*The "All's Well" Story from Boccaccio to Shakespeare* [Urbana, Ill.: University of Illinois Press, 1981], p. 131).

35. See John F. Adams, *"All's Well that Ends Well:* The Paradox of Procreation," *SQ* 12 (1961): 261–70.

36. See his famous introduction to *All's Well* (Cambridge: Cambridge University Press, 1929), p. xxxi. Quiller-Couch also found Helena very hard to take, calling her a "heroine of the pushing, calculating sort." His reaction is characteristic of many male critics, as well as others who dislike Helena's rise in social station: "Be it observed that all Shakespeare's heroines, save Helena, have royal or noble blood; that she alone belongs to what we call the upper-middle class; that the quarry on which Venus so ruthlessly attaches herself is a prey with two heads. She is perhaps too 'efficient' to engage our full sympathy" (see Clifford Leech, "The Theme of Ambition in *All's Well that Ends Well,*" *ELH* 21 [1954]: 17–29). If the reactions of Leech and Quiller-Couch are representative, we understand the wisdom of authors of the Griselda stories: clearly Helena does not suffer enough to earn her titled station. Apparently, the male may profit by marriage, if choosing or chosen, but the female may only profit if chosen.

37. See Joseph G. Price, *The Unfortunate Comedy* (Toronto: Toronto University Press, 1968).

38. Miles, *Problem,* pp. 125–60.

39. See note 24 for the editions of all these works.

40. John Marston, *The Fawn,* ed. G. A. Smith, Regents Series (Lincoln, Neb.: University of Nebraska Press, 1964).

41. Edward Sharpham, *The Fleire,* ed. Hunold Nibbe (1912; reprint, Vaduz: Kraus, 1963).

42. John Day, *Humour Out of Breath,* ed. J. O. Halliwell (London: Percy Library, 1860).

43. Thomas Dekker and John Webster, *West-Ward Hoe* (1607), Tudor Facsimile Reprints (New York: AMS Press, 1970).
44. John Marston, *The Malcontent,* ed. G. K. Hunter (Manchester: Manchester University Press, 1975).
45. Thomas Middleton, *The Phoenix* in *The Works of Thomas Middleton,* ed. A. H. Bullen (London: J. C. Nimmo, 1885).
46. John Day, *Law-tricks or Who would have thought it* in *The Works of John Day,* ed. A. H. Bullen (1881; reprint with introduction by Robin Jeffs, London: Holland Press, 1963).
47. Paul S. Seaver, Introduction to *Society in an Age of Revolution,* ed. Seaver (New York: Franklin Watts, 1976), p. 8.
48. Quoted in *ibid.,* p. 9.
49. See J. D. Chambers, "Population, Economy and Society," *Pre-Industrial England,* ed. W. A. Armstrong (Oxford: Oxford University Press, 1972), p. 27; D. C. Coleman, "Labour in the English Economy of the Seventeenth Century," *Society,* ed. Seaver, pp. 112–38.
50. William Harrison, *The Description of Britaine,* ed. Lothrop Withington (London: Walter Scott, 1889), p. 125.
51. *Seventeenth Century Economic Documents,* ed. Joan Thirsk and J. P. Cooper (Oxford: Clarendon Press, 1972), p. 117.
52. Robert Gray, *A Good Speed to Virginia* in *ibid.,* p. 757.
53. Statement of the King's Surveyor on enclosing forests and wastes (1612) in *ibid.,* p. 117.
54. John Howes, "Famyliar and Frendley Discourse Dialogue Wyse," (1587), *Tudor Economic Documents,* eds. R. H. Tawney and Eileen Power (1924; reprint, New York: Barnes and Noble, 1961), 3:421.
55. Edward Hext, "Letter to Burghley on the Increase of Rogues and Vagabonds" in *ibid.,* 2:342, 345–46.
56. Carl Bridenbaugh, *Vexed and Troubled Englishmen 1590–1642* (Oxford: Oxford University Press, 1967), pp. 40–41.
57. Peter Laslett, *Family Life and Illicit Love in Earlier Generations* (Cambridge: Cambridge University Press, 1977), p. 113.
58. Maurice Ashley, *The Stuarts in Love* (London: Hodder and Stoughton, 1963), p. 57.
59. Peter Laslett, "The Bastardy Prone Sub-society," *Bastardy and Its Comparative History,* ed. Peter Laslett, Karla Oostererveen, and Richard M. Smith (Cambridge, Mass.: Harvard University Press, 1980), pp. 217–46.
60. Thomas Nashe, *Christs Teares Over Ierusalem* (1593) (Menston: Scholar Press, 1970), and Thomas Dekker, *Lanthorne and Candle-Light* in *Non-Dramatic Works,* ed. Grosart, 3:175–303.
61. David Levine and Keith Wrightson, "The Social Context of Illegitimacy in Early Modern England," *Bastardy,* ed. Laslett *et al.,* pp. 170–72.
62. *Ibid.,* pp. 174–75.
63. Philip Stubbes, *The Anatomy of Abuses* (London: Richard Jones, 1583), chap. 3, n.p.
64. William Hunt, *The Puritan Moment: The Coming of Revolution in an English County* (Cambridge, Mass.: Harvard University Press, 1983), p. 76.
65. Emmison, *Disorder,* pp. 25ff.
66. Wallace Notestein, *The English People on the Eve of Colonization 1603–1630* (New York: Harper and Row, 1954), pp. 232–33.
67. *Tudor Economic Documents,* ed. Tawney and Power, 2:366.
68. Stubbes, *Anatomy,* chap. 3.
69. Quoted from Stubbes's *Anatomy of Abuses* in Edward Berry, *Shakespeare's Comic Rites* (Cambridge: Cambridge University Press, 1984), pp. 146–47.
70. Nashe, *Christs Teares,* p. 113.

71. In *Matrimoniall Honour: or, A Treatise of Marriage* (London: Th. Harper for Philip Newel, 1642) Daniel Rogers cautions his readers about marriage contracts because they are frequently broken if the conditions of the contract change. Alterations in fortune Rogers regards as poor reasons to break contracts, but he thinks one should break a contract with a party who has been incontinent before marriage (pp. 96–120).

72. See *Before the Bawdy Court,* ed. Paul Hair (London: Paul Elek, 1972), pp. 27–28.

73. Howes, "Discourse," *Tudor Documents,* 3:425.

74. Henry Arth, "Provision for the Poore," *Tudor Documents,* 2:453–54.

75. Hext, "To Burghley," *Tudor Documents,* 2:344.

76. *James I by His Contemporaries,* ed. Robert Ashton (London: Hutchinson, 1969), p. 6.

77. *Ibid.,* p. 10.

78. *Ibid.,* p. 66.

79. *A Jacobean Journal: Being a Record of Those Things Most Talked of During the Years 1603–1606,* ed. G. B. Harrison (London: George Routledge, 1941), pp. 86–89.

80. Lady Anne Clifford, *The Diary,* ed. Vita Sackville-West (New York: George Doran, 1923), pp. 16–17.

81. E. K. Chambers, *The Elizabethan Stage* (Oxford: Clarendon, 1923), 1:325.

82. Levine and Wrightson, "Social Context," pp. 173–74.

83. Joan Kent, "Attitudes of Members of the House of Commons to the Regulation of Personal Conduct in Late Elizabethan and Early Stuart England," *University of London Bulletin of the Institute of Historical Research* 46 (1973): 41–71.

84. *Ibid.,* p. 44.

85. *Ibid.,* p. 51.

86. *Ibid.,* p. 68.

87. *Ibid.,* p. 52.

88. Howes, "Discourse," *Tudor Documents,* 3:441–42.

89. Lawrence Stone, *The Causes of the English Revolution 1529–1642* (London: Routledge and Kegan Paul, 1972), pp. 76–77.

90. For comments on this theme see the discussion of *Measure* in Meredith A. Skura, *The Literary Use of the Psychoanalytic Process* (New Haven, Conn.: Yale University Press, 1981).

91. Franco Moretti, "'A Huge Eclipse': Tragic Form and the Deconsecration of Sovereignty," *Genre* 15 (1982): 23.

92. See Jonathan Goldberg, who says, "the Duke's wooing of Isabella, even though he offers marriage, seems at least as much an assault upon her integrity as Angelo's proposition" (*James I and the Politics of Literature* [Baltimore, Md.: Johns Hopkins University Press, 1983], p. 235).

93. Richard Wheeler, *Shakespeare's Development and the Problem Comedies: Turn and Counter-Turn* (Berkeley: University of California Press, 1981), p. 139. For an extended discussion of the complexities of the Duke's character, see Miles, *Problem,* pp. 161–96.

94. See Leonard Tennenhouse, "Representing Power: *Measure for Measure* in Its Time," *Genre* 15 (1982): 139–56. This discussion relates the figure of the Duke to the traditional trickster.

95. Goldberg's arguments demonstrate the sense in which the Jacobean ideology is based on invasion, as we would see it, of the personal by the state, "that the body is consumed for the sake of ideology" (*James I,* p. 88). He says, "Donne's lovers in bed alone; Donne himself in bed in illness; Stuart families in the intimacy of marriage, procreation, and death: the net of political discourse encompasses this territory" (p. 55).

96. *Works of James,* ed. McIlwain, p. 3. Goldberg discusses "the stile of *Gods*" at length (pp. 27–54).

97. The concept of *arcana imperii,* secrets of state, is constantly invoked in Jacobean

rhetoric to justify royal secretiveness, absence from office, and even princely disguise (see Goldberg, "State Secrets," in *James I* pp. 69–85).

98. Again, neither James, nor those who accept his rhetoric, would experience this disquiet.

99. See Moretti, who says, "Beginning with the figure of the protagonist, the legitimate holder of supreme authority, Shakespeare's Duke or Marston's Altofront, we notice that his fundamental characteristic is *not to be subject to the passions.* This separates him from the other characters, who are notably weaker in this respect, and designates him as the sovereign of the Elizabethan utopia, dedicated to the public weal insofar as devoid of personal interests" (p. 21).

100. See Goldberg, who remarks, "No exact replay of James at all, the play yet manages to catch at central concerns: in the disguised Duke, the king's divided self; in the relations between privacy and the public, the play between internal and external theaters of conscience; in the Duke's actions, the combination of absence and presence through which James claimed authority" (p. 235).

101. Goldberg says, "the Duke, who professes complete power and control, is not in fact all-powerful. Lucio's accusations have force; the Duke's plots cause us discomfort and strain our credulity, too. Yet the Duke even asserts control over what he cannot control" (p. 235).

Chapter Three

1. Jonathan Goldberg, *James I and the Politics of Literature* (Baltimore, Md.: Johns Hopkins University Press, 1983), p. 240.

2. David Bevington, ed., *The Complete Works of Shakespeare,* 3d ed. (Glenview, Ill.: Scott, Foresman, 1980), p. 1414.

3. Roland Barthes, "Myth Today" in *A Barth Reader,* ed. Susan Sontag (New York: Hill and Wang, 1982), pp. 116, 132.

4. See Stephen Orgel, *The Illusion of Power: Political Theater in the English Renaissance* (Berkeley, Calif.: University of California Press, 1975); Goldberg, *James I,* pp. 113–47; D. J. Gordon, *The Renaissance Imagination: Essays and Lectures,* ed. Stephen Orgel (Berkeley, Calif.: University of California Press, 1975), *passim.*

5. John W. Allen, *A History of Political Thought in the Sixteenth Century* (London: Methuen, 1928), p. 249.

6. See Gordon Schochet, *Patriarchalism in Political Thought: The Authoritarian Family and Political Speculation and Attitudes, Especially in Seventeenth-Century England* (Oxford: Blackwell, 1975), chap. 1; W. H. Greenleaf, *Order, Empiricism, and Politics: Two Traditions of English Political Thought, 1500–1700* (Oxford: Oxford University Press, 1964); R. W. K. Hinton, "Husbands, Fathers and Conquerors," *Political Studies* 15 (1967): 291–300, and 16 (1968): 55–67.

7. Richard Hooker, *Of the Laws of Ecclesiastical Polity* in *The Works of Richard Hooker,* ed. W. Speed Hill, Folger Edition (Cambridge: Harvard University Press, 1981), 1.12.

8. John Overall, *Convocation Book of 1606* (Oxford: Parker, 1844), p. 8.

9. *The Political Works of James I,* ed. C. H. McIlwain (Cambridge, Mass.: Harvard University Press, 1918), pp. 55, 308.

10. Richard Mocket, *God and the King* (London: His Majestes command, 1615), p. 79.

11. Edward Coke, *Posnati,* Calvin Case, VII, *Coke Reports* 12 (1606); quoted by Gordon Schochet, "Patriarchalism, Politics and Mass Attitudes in Stuart England," *Historical Journal* 12 (1969): 438.

12. Edward Forset, *A Comparative Discourse of the Bodies Natural and Politique* (London: I. Bill, 1606), pp. 57, 29–30.

13. See Schochet, *Patriarchalism*, pp. 54–55.

14. A. O. Lovejoy and George Boas, *Primitivism and Related Ideas in Antiquity* (1935; reprint, New York: Octagon Books, 1965), p. 12.

15. Carolyn Merchant, *The Death of Nature: Women, Ecology, and the Scientific Revolution* (New York: Harper and Row, 1980), pp. 6, 7.

16. Lovejoy and Boas, *Primitivism*, p. 448, no. 15; Merchant, *Death*, p. 7.

17. Thomas G. Rosenmeyer, *The Green Cabinet: Theocritus and the European Pastoral Lyric* (Berkeley, Calif.: University of California Press, 1969), p. 19.

18. For many meanings of this complex term, see Paul Alpers, "What Is Pastoral?" *CI* 8 (1982): 437–60. Alpers argues that "pastoral works are representations of shepherds, who are felt to be representative of some other or of all men" (p. 456). And further that "certain kinds of landscape are the setting in which shepherds lead their lives" (p. 459).

19. Merchant, *Death*, p. 73.

20. See Schochet, *Patriarchalism*, chap. 2, and Greenleaf, *Order*, chap. 2.

21. Merchant, *Death*, pp. 76, 79.

22. See "Some Paradoxes of Utopia" in Harry Levin, *The Myth of the Golden Age in the Renaissance* (Bloomington, Ind.: Indiana University Press, 1969), pp. 187–93.

23. The concepts of romance employed here are shaped by Northrop Frye, *Anatomy of Criticism: Four Essays* (Princeton, N.J.: Princeton University Press, 1957), pp. 186–206; and Frederic R. Jameson, "Magical Narratives," *NLH* 7 (1975–76): 135–63.

24. See James Siemon, "Noble Virtue in *Cymbeline*," *ShS* 29 (1976): 51–62, for a full discussion of the interesting doubles in this play.

25. See Derek Traversi, *Shakespeare: The Last Phase* (Stanford, Calif.: Stanford University Press, 1965), p. 46.

26. In "An Interpretation of Pastoral in *The Winter's Tale*," *SQ* 22 (1971), Philip Weinstein says, "Art, then, in *The Winter's Tale* is simultaneously natural (Polixenes's theory) and artificial (Perdita's theory). There is both idealism and realism, art and the mockery (which marks the limitations) of art. The more comprehensive realism effected by this combination is the governing principle of the Pastoral Scene. Ultimately, constancy within time, abiding value that is both proved and used within flux, is the only possible victory that is convincing. Convincing because it admits its loss" (p. 109). See also, Peter Lindenbaum, "Time, Sexual Love, and the Uses of the Pastoral in *The Winter's Tale*," *MLQ* 33 (1972): 3–22.

27. For an excellent analysis of these works see Wayne Shumaker, *The Occult Sciences in the Renaissance: A Study in Intellectual Patterns* (Berkeley, Calif.: University of California Press, 1972), pp. 108–56. Shumaker distinguishes among natural magic, spiritual magic, and astrological magic as subdivisions of white magic. Prospero seems to use all three as Kermode has shown in *The Tempest*, ed. Frank Kermode, Arden Edition (New York: Random House, 1964), pp. xl–xli, xlviii–li. My disagreements with Kermode will emerge at the end of the chapter.

28. Merchant, *Death*, p. 106.

29. See Shumaker, *Sciences*, chap. 2.

30. L. T. Fitz, "The Vocabulary of the Environment in *The Tempest*," *SQ* 26 (1975): 42–47.

31. Eleanor T. Lincoln, *Pastoral and Romance: Modern Essays in Criticism* (Englewood Cliffs, N.J.: Prentice-Hall, 1969), p. 2. Lincoln says, "The essentials that shape the pastoral are withdrawal to a place apart and from that place a perspective of what man has made of man. . . . Shepherd and reader re-emerge from the place apart to return, strengthened and enlightened, to active engagement in the imperfect world. The return distinguishes significant pastoral."

32. See Fitz, "Vocabulary," pp. 42–43.
33. This is Coppèlia Kahn's phrase from *Man's Estate: Masculine Identity in Shakespeare* (Berkeley, Calif.: University of California Press, 1981), p. 220.
34. William Perkins, *Workes* (London: I. Legatt, 1609–12), 1:763.
35. Lawrence Stone, "Social Mobility in England, 1500–1700," *Seventeenth-Century England: Society in an Age of Revolution*, ed. Paul Seaver (New York: Franklin Watts, 1976), p. 37.
36. Francis Markham, *The Book of Honour* (London: A. Matthewes and J. Norton, 1625), p. 48.
37. Sir Thomas Smith, *De Republica Anglorum*, ed. Mary Dewar (Cambridge: Cambridge University Press, 1982), pp. 70–72.
38. Mervyn James, *Family, Lineage, and Civil Society: A Study of Society, Politics, and Mentality in the Durham Region, 1500–1640* (Oxford: Clarendon Press, 1974), pp. 67–107.
39. Baldesare Castiglione, *The Book of the Courtier*, trans. Charles Singleton (New York: Anchor Books, 1959), pp. 28–32.
40. Sir Thomas Elyot, *The Boke named The Governour*, ed. H. S. Croft (1883; reprint, New York: Burt Franklin, 1967), 2:26.
41. Lawrence Humphrey, *The Nobles or Of Nobility* (London: Thomas Marshe, 1563), sig. ci.
42. Ruth Kelso, *The Institution of the Gentleman in English Literature of the Sixteenth Century* (Urbana, Ill.: University of Illinois, 1923), p. 7.
43. See Goldberg's analysis of representations of the family in seventeenth-century paintings in *James I*, pp. 90–107.
44. Kermode, Arden *Tempest*, pp. liv–lix.
45. Edmund Spenser, *The Fairie Queene* in *The Poetical Works*, ed. J. C. Smith and E. DeSelincourt (Oxford: Oxford University Press, 1947), 6.5.1. See also Lila Geller, "Spenser's Theory of Nobility in Book VI of *The Fairie Queene*," *ELR* 5 (1975): 49–57.
46. Goldberg, *James I*, p. 12.
47. William Harrison, *The Description of Britaine*, ed. Lothrop Withington (London: Walter Scott, 1889), pp. 118–19.
48. Mildred Campbell, *The English Yeoman under Elizabeth and the Early Stuarts* (New Haven: Yale University Press, 1942), pp. 186–87.
49. W. G. Hoskins, "The Rebuilding of Rural England, 1570–1640," *Past and Present* 4 (1953): 44–59.
50. D. C. Coleman, *The Economy of England 1450–1750* (Oxford: Oxford University Press, 1977), pp. 45–46.
51. Harrison, *Description*, p. 120.
52. Francis Bacon, "Of the true Greatness of Kingdoms," *Essays, Advancement of Learning, New Atlantis and Other Pieces*, ed. R. F. Jones (New York: Odyssey Press, 1937), pp. 86–87.
53. John Fletcher, "To the Reader," *The Faithful Shepherdess, The Dramatic Works of the Beaumont and Fletcher Canon*, ed. Fredson Bowers (Cambridge: Cambridge University Press, 1976), 3:497.
54. Sir Thomas Wilson, *The State of England 1600* in *Seventeenth-Century Economic Documents*, ed. Joan Thirsk and J. P. Cooper (Oxford: Clarendon, 1972), p. 752; Stone, "Social Mobility," p. 43.
55. See *The Winter's Tale*, ed. J. H. P. Pafford, Arden Edition (London: Methuen, 1963), notes to 4.4.337–39 (p. 110).
56. In *The Myth of the Golden Age* Harry Levin says, "This is the dilemma of authority, which either keeps the ideal commonwealth from coming into existence or else keeps existing commonwealths from ever becoming ideal. The best regimes have traced their institutions back, through the convenient obscurity of the legendary past, to some wise lawgiver" (p. 187).

57. Thomas Becon, *A New Catechisme Sette Forth Dialogewise in familiare talke between the father and the son*, ed. John Ayre (Cambridge: Parker Society, 1844), p. 88.

58. Schochet, *Patriarchalism*, p. 55.

59. Jean Bodin, *The Six Bookes of a Commonweale*, ed. K. D. McRae, Facsimile of English Translation of 1606 (Cambridge, Mass.: Harvard University Press, 1962), p. 7.

60. Robert Filmer, *Patriarcha with Two Treatises of Government by John Locke*, ed. Thomas I. Cooke (New York: Hafer, 1947), p. 255.

61. Thomas Bilson, *The True Difference Between Christian Subjection and Unchristian Rebellion* (1585), p. 251. Quoted in Charles H. George and Katherine George, *The Protestant Mind of the English Reformation 1570–1649* (Princeton, N.J.: Princeton University Press, 1961), p. 185.

62. Schochet, *Patriarchalism*, p. 43.

63. Michael Walzer, *The Revolution of the Saints: A Study in the Origins of Radical Politics* (Cambridge, Mass.: Harvard University Press, 1965), p. 49.

64. William Perkins, *Christian Oeconomie*, trans. T. Pickering (London: E. Weaver, 1609), pp. 163–64.

65. *The Politics of Johannes Althusius*, trans. and ed. Frederick S. Carney (Boston, Mass.: Beacon Press, 1964), pp. 22–27.

66. Bodin, *Commonweale*, pp. 14–19, 20.

67. Francis Bacon, *New Atlantis* in *Essays*, ed. Jones, pp. 471–72, 475.

68. Goldberg, *James I*, p. 99.

69. Although Stone describes the seventeenth-century family in England as the restricted Patriarchal Nuclear Family in *Family, Sex and Marriage 1500–1800* (New York: Harper and Row, 1977), p. 218, and Steven Ozment has more recently studied the patriarchal family in Germany (*When Fathers Ruled: Family Life in Reformation Europe* [Cambridge, Mass.: Harvard University Press, 1983]), there is too much variation among the political theories and local family structures to justify the easy conclusion that the theories reproduce the social order, especially if one allows for class and religious differences. See Keith Wrightson, *English Society 1580–1680* (New Brunswick, N.J.: Rutgers University Press, 1982).

70. R. M. K. Hinton, "Husbands, Fathers and Conquerors," *Political Studies* 15 (1967): 292.

71. *Works of James*, ed. McIlwain, p. 308.

72. Bodin, *Commonweale*, pp. 20–21.

73. Hinton, "Husbands," p. 294.

74. See Peter Erickson, who says, "This mirroring of the father in the son provides the basis for the transmission of property, values, and the self (since the son reincarnates the father). It ensures the continuity and self-perpetuation of the patriarchal order. The son is the lifeblood of the system, its source of rejuvenation" ("Patriarchal Structures in *The Winter's Tale*," *PMLA* 97 [1982]: 821).

75. Carol T. Neely, "Women and Issue in *The Winter's Tale*," *PQ* 57 (1978): 181. Lindenbaum connects these attitudes to the pastoral: see note 26.

76. "Because Hermione's and Leontes' respective roles as all-giving and all-worshipping are fixed, their newly won mutuality is stereotypical. The exchange comprises Hermione's conferring sustenance and forgiveness on Leontes and his conferring appreciative idealization on her. His idolatry, however, needs to be placed in its larger context of patriarchal ideology, for such worship does not prevent Leontes from resuming political control" (Erickson, "Patriarchal Structures," p. 826).

77. Charles Frey, "O sacred, shadowy, cold and constant queen': Shakespeare's Imperiled and Chastening Daughters of Romance," *The Woman's Part: Feminist Criticism of Shakespeare*, ed. Carolyn R. S. Lenz, Gayle Greene, and Carol T. Neely (Urbana, Ill.: University of Illinois Press, 1980), p. 308.

78. Meredith Skura discusses the psychological effects of Posthumus's dream in "Interpreting Posthumus' Dream from Above and Below," *Representing Shakespeare: New Psychoanalytic Essays,* ed. Murray Schwartz and Coppèlia Kahn (Baltimore, Md.: Johns Hopkins University Press, 1980), pp. 203–16.

79. Kahn says, "He breaks out of repetition, out of the revenge cycle and out of his oedipal past. But he also fails to recreate in any mature sexual relationship the life giving love experience first known with the mother" (*Man's Estate,* p. 223).

80. Kermode says, "In an age when 'natural' conduct was fashionably associated with sexual promiscuity, chastity alone could stand as the chief function of temperance, and there is considerable emphasis on this particular restraint in *The Tempest.* The practice of good magic required it" (Arden *Tempest,* p. xlix). See also Shumaker, *Sciences,* for the reference to Agrippa (p. 146).

81. John Hayward, *An Answer to the First Part of a Certain Conference, Concerning Succession,* Facsimile of 1603 edition (Norwood, N.J.: W. J. Johnson, 1975), sig. C4.

82. Ernst H. Kantorowicz, *The King's Two Bodies: A Study in Medieval Political Theology* (Princeton, N.J.: Princeton University Press, 1957); Marie Axton, *The Queen's Two Bodies: Drama and the Elizabethan Succession* (London: Royal Historical Society, 1977).

83. Hooker, *Ecclesiastical Polity* in *The Works of Richard Hooker,* ed. Hill, 8.2.9–10.

84. *Works of James,* ed. McIlwain, p. 273.

85. *Ibid.,* p. 3.

86. Ben Jonson, *Prince Henry's Barriers* in *The Complete Masques,* ed. Stephen Orgel (New Haven, Conn.: Yale University Press, 1969), ll. 407–11.

87. Goldberg, *James I,* pp. 84–85; G. R. Elton says, "The one question left open in Tudor divine right teaching was this: who is the king appointed by God? The Tudor answer was pragmatic: whoever happens to be recognized as king. Anything more philosophical would have been awkward for a dynasty whose original claim was very weak, and which encountered a series of succession problems. But the Stuarts, safer in their descent and happier in their production of progeny, felt able to claim that God's choice was announced by birth: at any given moment, there was always one true king, whether or not he in fact ever managed to sit on a throne, and he was his predecessor's legitimate heir" (*Studies in Tudor and Stuart Politics and Government: Papers and Reviews 1946–72* [Cambridge: Cambridge University Press, 1974], p. 204).

88. "After a few years, when we had experience of the Scottish government, then in disparagement of the Scots, and in hate and detestation of them, the queen did seem to revive; then was her memory much magnified—such ringing of bells, such public joy and sermons in commemoration of her, the picture of her tomb painted in many churches, and in effect more solemnity and joy in memory of her coronation than was for the coming of King James" (Godfrey Goodman in *James I by his Contemporaries,* p. 77).

89. Frances A. Yates, *Shakespeare's Last Plays: A New Approach* (London: Routlege and Kegan Paul, 1975), p. 32.

90. Lisa Jardine, *Still Harping on Daughters: Women and Drama in the Age of Shakespeare* (Sussex: Harvester Press, 1983), p. 85.

91. Jardine cites the work of Stanley Chojnacki about wills of Venetian noblewomen in "Patrician Women in Early Renaissance Venice," *Studies in the Renaissance* 21 (1974): 176–203; see also his article, "Dowries and Kinsmen in Early Renaissance Venice," *Women in Medieval Society,* ed. S. M. Stuard (Philadelphia: University of Pennsylvania Press, 1976), pp. 173–98.

92. Cyrus Hoy, "Fathers and Daughters in Shakespeare's Romances," *Shakespeare's Romances Reconsidered,* ed. Carol Kay and Henry Jacobs (Lincoln, Neb.: University of Nebraska Press, 1978), pp. 77–90, and C. L. Barber, "'Thou That Beget'st Him That Did Thee Beget': Transformation in Pericles and *The*

Winter's Tale," ShS 22 (1969): 59–67. Kahn remarked: "The shift from twin to daughter as the figure through whom the hero gains his final identity is crucial. What it means is that he breaks out of time conceived as a repetition of oedipal patterns and breaks into the future through his daughter and his own, new family" (*Man's Estate*, p. 213).

93. "The reconcilation of father and daughter precedes that of husband and wife partially because the former provides a comfortable and stable means of re-covering a positive feminine image. The father-daughter relation is clearly hierarchical and therefore less threatening to the male" (Erickson, "Patriarchal Structures," pp. 825–26).

94. Bodin, *Commonweale*, p. 21.

95. *Ibid.*, p. 23.

96. C. N. Agrippa, *Of the Nobilitie and Excellencie of Womankynde* (London: Thomas Berthelet, 1542), Sig. Ciir.

97. Christine de Pizan, *The Book of the City of Ladies*, trans. E. J. Richards (New York: Persea Books, 1982), II.ll.1–2; pp. 115–16; *An Apologie for Woman-kinde* (London: Edward Allde for William Ferebrand, 1605), Sig. C3r; and Thomas Heywood, *Gynaikeion or Nine Books of various history Concerning women* (London: A. Islip, 1624), p. 320.

98. Feminists have often perceived this feature of modern authoritarian regimes. Jane Marcus shows how Virginia Woolf sensed this connection between fascist regimes and motherhood when she wrote *Three Guineas*. (See "Liberty, So-rority, Misogyny," *The Representation of Women in Fiction*, ed. Carolyn Heilbrun and Margaret Higonnet (Baltimore, Md.: Johns Hopkins University Press, 1983), pp. 60–97.) The best single essay on the subject is the brilliant and enigmatic one by Maria-Antoinetta Macciocchi, "Female Sexuality in Fascist Ideology," *Feminist Review* 1 (1979): 67–82. Kahn says of Marina and Perdita, "They then function as mothers do to their fathers by 'delivering' them to new identities as fathers. They also serve as doubles of their mothers, uniting chas-tity with fertility and countering their mothers' oedipally tinged sexuality" (*Man's Estate*, p. 221).

99. Goldberg, *James I*, p. 101.

100. Bacon, *New Atlantis*, pp. 475–76.

101. Barber, "Thou That Beget'st Him," p. 61.

102. Forset, *Comparative Discourse*, pp. 33–34.

103. Kantorowicz, *Two Bodies*, pp. 394–95.

104. Goldberg, *James I*, p. 97.

105. *Works of James*, ed. McIlwain, p. 55.

106. James, *Family, Lineage*, p. 192.

107. Spenser, *Fairie Queene*, 6.10.23.

108. *Works of James*, ed. McIlwain, p. 307.

109. Stephen Orgel, *The Illusion of Power: Political Theater in the English Renaissance* (Berkeley, Calif.: University of California Press, 1975), p. 52.

110. Goldberg, *James I*, pp. 123–31.

111. Jonson, *Oberon* in *Complete Masques*, ed. Orgel, ll. 267–74.

112. Kermode, Arden *Tempest*, p. xli n. 5.

113. Goldberg, *James I*, p. 99.

114. D. J. Gordon, "*Hymenai:* Ben Jonson's Masque of Union," *Renaissance Imagina-tion*, ed. Orgel, pp. 168–74.

115. *Works of James*, ed. McIlwain, p. 271.

116. Quoted in George and George, *Protestant Mind*, p. 219.

117. *Works of James*, ed. McIlwain, pp. 271–72.

118. Gordon, "*Hymenai:* Ben Jonson's Masque of Union," *Renaissance Imagination*, ed. Orgel, p. 174.

119. Jonson, *Complete Masques*, ed. Orgel, ll. 335–38.

120. Markham, *Honour*, pp. 199–200.

121. See Bernard Harris, "'What's past is prologue': *Cymbeline* and *Henry VIII*," *Later Shakespeare*, ed. J. R. Brown and Bernard Harris, Stratford-upon-Avon Studies, vol. 8 (London: Edward Arnold, 1966), pp. 217–23. Harris relates the image to Stuart masques and political ideas. For a critique of such approaches to the romances, see Hallett Smith, *Shakespeare's Romances: A Study of Some Ways of the Imagination* (San Marino, Calif.: Huntington Library, 1972), pp. 211–21.

122. Josephine Waters Bennett, "Britain Among the Fortunate Isles," *SP* 53 (1956): 114–40.

123. See *Complete Masques*, p. 473, for Orgel's note; *Masque of Blackness*, l. 218; *Love Freed from Ignorance and Folly*, l. 241; *Masque of Queens*, l. 371; *Pleasure Reconciled*, l. 178; *Fortunate Isles*, passim.

124. See Harry Berger, Jr., "Miraculous Harp: A Reading of Shakespeare's *Tempest*" *ShakS* 5 (1970): 253–68. Berger says, "He finds that magic cannot save souls, cannot even pinch the will. More than this, he finds that magic is the only effective policeman" (p. 269).

125. Here I disagree with Kermode, who sees Prospero as already possessing self-governance in his role as magician: "The self-discipline of the magician is the self-discipline of the prince" (p. xlix).

126. Goldberg, *James I*, p. 31.

127. William Matchett, "Some Dramatic Techniques in 'The Winter's Tale,'" *ShS* 22 (1969): 99.

128. Arthur C. Kirsch, "*Cymbeline* and Coterie Dramaturgy," *ELH* 34 (1967): 285–306, and Roger Warren, "Theatrical Virtuosity and Poetic Complexity in *Cymbeline*," *ShS* 29 (1976): 41–50.

129. Warren, "Theatrical Virtuosity," p. 41; Kirsch, "*Cymbeline* and Coterie Dramaturgy," p. 295.

130. Leonard Powlick, "*Cymbeline* and the Comedy of Anti-climax," *Shakespeare's Last Plays*, ed. R. C. Tobias and P. G. Zolbrod (Athens, Ohio: Ohio University Press, 1974), pp. 131–41, and Robert Uphaus, *Beyond Tragedy: Structure and Experience in Shakespeare's Romances* (Lexington, Ky.: University of Kentucky Press, 1981), pp. 49–69.

131. Matchett, "Some Dramatic Techniques," pp. 102, 106, 101.

Epilogue

1. Michael Foucault, *The History of Sexuality, Volume I: An Introduction*, trans. Robert Hurley (New York: Vintage, 1980), pp. 91, 92–93, 86.

2. *Ibid.*, pp. 155, 156.

3. *Ibid.*, pp. 105–6.

4. *Ibid.*, p. 144.

5. Michael Foucault, *Discipline and Punish: The Birth of the Prison*, trans. Alan Sheridan (New York: Vintage, 1979), pp. 195–228.

6. Foucault, *History of Sexuality*, p. 146.

7. *Ibid.*, pp. 106, 108.

8. See Elizabeth Janeway, who says, "The chastity of women is an ideal enforced, not simply by a patriarchal social structure, but also by a society in which legitimate inheritance of property is a matter of enormous economic importance. It is the latter factor whose significance has waned. Patriarchy is still with us, but the economic function of chastity is vanishing" ("Who Is Sylvia? On the

Loss of Sexual Paradigms," *Signs: Journal of Women in Culture and Society* 5, no. 4 [Summer, 1980]: 583). Janeway foresees the need for new paradigms of female sexuality, but acknowledges the endurance of patriarchal attitudes. I would emphasize here the continued male need to control reproduction in the presence of changed economic, social, and political conditions, as well as new medical technologies.

INDEX

Marilyn L. Williamson is professor of English and director of Women's Studies at Wayne State University. She previously taught at Duke University, North Carolina State University, and Oakland University. She received her M.A. degree from the University of Wisconsin and her Ph.D. from Duke University. Dr. Williamson has written Infinite Variety: Antony and Cleopatra in Renaissance Drama and Earlier Tradition and edited Frederic Rowton's Female Poets of Great Britain in addition to publishing numerous articles in scholarly journals.

The manuscript was edited by Anne M. G. Adamus. The book was designed by Don Ross. The typeface for the text is Baskerville, based on the original design by John Baskerville in the eighteenth century. The typefaces for the display are Arnold Bocklin and Friz Quadrata. The book is printed on 60-lb. Glatfelter and bound in Holliston's Roxite Linen over binder's boards.
Manufactured in the United States of America.